Through Hope's Eyes

Mary V. Young

Through Hope's Eyes

ISBN 978-1-304-57838-9

Fiwitt Enterprises

First Print Edition

Cover design: http://digitaldonna.com

Dedicated
to the One
who gives me the stories

Acknowledgements

Acknowledgements aren't always about thanking people who helped you write a book -- sometimes they're about thanking people who helped you change your life, which ultimately helped you write a book. For me, some of those people are **Esther Lutze, Chuck Rivers, Marge Robertson, and LouJeanne Walton**, who always saw me *Through Love's Eyes*, which helped me see my world *Through Hope's Eyes*. I thank God that their lives touched mine.

My editor, **Sharon Brown**, continues to challenge and encourage me, as well.

When I started writing this book, I asked God for a writing partner. Since God doesn't always work in traditional ways, I wasn't surprised that the writing partner he sent me was most definitely *not* a traditional writing partner. I thank Him daily for my wonderful massage therapist, **Shannon Pengitore** -- I've lost track of how many plot points were worked out while I was on her massage table. Shannon, you may not consider yourself a writer, but you've been a fantastic writing partner for me. Thanks for massaging my story ideas as well as my muscles.

I also need to give a shout-out to **Pastor Gerald Ripley and the members of Abundant Life Church in San Antonio, TX**. This was my church home in the 1990s, and they loved me as I was, while encouraging me to grow as a Christian, a human being, and a writer. Some of the stories in this book began as Christmas recitations there.

And an extra special thank you to **Jeff Jackson of Watermarke Church in Woodstock GA,** for turning my entire understanding of the nativity on its head, as well as for time spent clarifying Biblical concepts and historical points. Any errors or inaccuracies are my fault, not his.

Stories

Stories

An Attack

I curled into myself, my screams dying to moans. Nothing I could do would change anything. My son was dead, killed by a soldier's sword. The dry street grew muddy beneath my face. My husband's hands were gentle as he lifted me, carried me into the house; then lay me on our bed.

I wish I need never leave here. I wish I could spend the rest of my life hiding from this truth. But I cannot hide: my mind keeps reliving the horror, beginning with the pounding on our door.

When Ari opened it, two soldiers pushed him aside, one drawing his sword as he entered. The other spoke a command that froze my heart. By the order of King Herod, my baby must die. Screaming, I threw myself at the soldier who was reaching for my precious son. His fist in my stomach stole my breath. By the time I could breathe again, our door was closing behind them. Ari tried to hold me, but I pulled free and ran outside. The street was crowded with soldiers holding boys of all ages from newborn to toddler. I could not see my son, but when I screamed his name, I heard his answering cry. Other mothers were searching as I was, and the combination of our screams and the babies' cries was deafening.

Those soldiers not holding our sons formed a living wall, barricading us from our hearts. I tried pleading with one, but his face was impassive; his eyes looking above and beyond us, staring into the distance. I pushed him, but it was like pushing a stone wall. Even hitting and kicking him had no effect.

Our sons were screaming their fear and confusion, and then suddenly -- they weren't. The only sound was the mothers' voices as they called their sons' names. The soldiers melted away from in front of us, and I screamed until I had no voice. I wanted to run to my son, but could not move. My knees buckled, and I curled into myself on the ground, my screams dying to moans.

When I am not reliving the event, I am asking questions that have no answers. *"How can Yahweh ever be glorified by this slaughter?"* Did my ancestors wonder the same thing when Pharaoh was killing their children? Papa had always told us the Passover story was about hope, not despair. But where was the hope in this?

How do I explain to my daughters? How do I sleep when every time I close my eyes, I see their faces, feel the soldier's fist in my stomach? I wish they were animals, wish they had been brutes. But they were soldiers following orders, their faces as calm as on a parade ground.

I don't want it to be real. I want to wake up to little Ari's voice asking another thousand questions as he explores our world, but I'll never hear him again. I don't know how to keep going on; don't know why I should. I didn't know I could hurt so much without physical injury, and I don't know if this pain will ever go away.

If Papa were here, he would help me make sense of it, like he helped us understand Pharaoh. He would tell me that Yahweh has some greater plan beyond my ability to see. But he is not here, and I lie alone in the darkness of my heart, empty arms aching to be filled.

As my father told the story, the hair on my arms stood up, and I breathed faster. It didn't matter that I knew it by heart. I always had the same reaction.

"Why, Papa?" My younger brother asked. "Why was the

Pharaoh so mean?"

I whispered Papa's answer along with him. "Yahweh hardened Pharaoh's heart, my son."

"But why, Papa? Why would he do that?"

Again, I whispered Papa's answer. "Pharaoh did not believe in the One True God. Yahweh used our trials and the Pharaoh's punishment to reveal His glory and power."

*The questions and answers were part of the story for us, as much a ritual as the night of remembrance the story led to. This was the story of Moshe, used by Yahweh to lead us out of Egypt and into our promised land. That year, the story hit me harder -- that year, I was old enough to bear children, and when Papa told the part about Pharaoh killing the baby boys, I couldn't breathe. What would I do, I wondered, if soldiers came to take **my** baby boy?*

"Miriam, are you all right?"

"Papa, what could we do if someone came to take our babies? What would it feel like?"

"I pray you never have to know, little girl." Papa's hand was gentle as he stroked my hair.

"Please Yahweh," I prayed silently. "Protect all your children, and keep them safe."

Papa was long-gone, and Mama was a grandmother several times over. I was a mama now, my girls healthy and growing strong. But no boys. I had never been able to carry a boy to delivery.

Until now. When the ladies told me I had a son, I wept from joy. Now Ari would have someone to carry on his work. As I fed my son, I dreamt of the day he would work beside his father, his young strength making Ari strong.

Ari wept too, when he held his son for the first time. As I fell asleep that night, the prayer from my childhood floated through my mind. *"Please Yahweh, protect all your children, and keep them safe."*

Any baby brought joy to our household, but with little Ari it was tripled. His sisters delighted in helping to care for him, sometimes arguing over whose turn it was. I watched every milestone with a sad joy. He rolled over; he crawled; he pulled himself up onto his knees; he stood; he tottered forward, grinning so hugely we couldn't help but laugh at his joy.

My baby boy -- the last baby I would have -- was growing up. Soon he would be a boy, not a baby. He would grow in stature and strength, learning about Yahweh, following his father, one day becoming a father himself. These were my dreams for him, so vivid they felt like reality.

Those dreams are dry dust now, crushed under a soldier's foot, washed away in a flood of tears along a river of blood dripping from a soldier's sword. I no longer wonder what it would feel like if soldiers came to take my baby boy. Now I wonder how I will continue when the heart has been ripped from my chest. I wonder how Yahweh could be so cruel; how Herod could be so evil.

HE WAS A BABY!

Not even two years old -- how could he ever threaten a king?

Did Yahweh harden Herod's heart like he did Pharaoh? How did my ancestors trust Yahweh after that? How could I? But how could I not? He is Yahweh -- his ways are foreign to us. He moves the stars in the sky, brings the rain for our crops. He fed us in the desert, delivered us from Pharaoh's hand. He is the God who keeps his promises, and that truth stretches back through all the generations of our people. Losing my son must be part of some greater plan I cannot see. But what plan could Yahweh have that requires mothers' hearts to break?

Esther worries about me, but I cannot rouse myself to reassure her. I cannot do anything, except cry and sleep. How many tears does one heart hold? Is it possible to die from grief, to cry oneself to death? I don't know -- I only know that my eyes are red and sore, and that my tears do not wash away my pain.

Mama brings me food, but when I try to eat, it tastes like sand and I leave most of it untouched. Ari mourns too, but it is different for men. He didn't carry our son inside his body for nine months, feeling him grow right beneath his heart.

I close my eyes against the daylight and wander the night time in my soul, where no stars light the darkness and Yahweh ignores his promises. I know I am wrong to think this way, but it feels as if I am some other person; not the Miriam I have always been, but a bitter, disillusioned woman who has no more heart for life.

Mama sits with me, but her murmured reassurances cannot pierce my darkness. A corner of my mind tries to tell me that grief is a luxury we cannot afford, but it makes no difference. I am lost in the darkness that covered me when I saw his lifeless body, and there is no way out. Mama's soothing voice is a gentle river current flowing through my mind, telling me the ordinary stories of our village, or the gossip from the well. I hear, but at the same time I do not hear, her voice forming a backdrop to my memories.

Little Ari, wrinkled and red after his first breath, tiny hands swinging before he was swaddled. Those same hands, larger now, clapping along as we sing songs, his face broken in two by his grin. Following his sisters as fast as his little legs would carry him, picking himself up every time he fell down. I did not know heartache could be physical, but mine is an ache in my chest that will not ease; a heaviness that steals my breath.

I wish Papa were here to make sense of this for me. Maybe he could explain the kind of world where a king is allowed to kill babies.

Mama's voice continued outside my pain, telling of a flower Esther saw on a walk, blooming in the crevice of a rock. The fields were ripe with grain, she said; it would soon be harvest time. In my mind, I saw sunshine gilding the grain sheaves, heard the laughter of the children celebrating a successful harvest. Little Ari was born during harvest time...

My tears puddled beneath my face: Mama sat beside me stroking my matted hair, while an animal howled in the distance.

It gets better with time, they tell me, but I'm not sure that's true. Will time make sense out of this senseless slaughter? Will time tell our village why our sons had to die?

Yahweh is all knowing and all powerful, but he keeps his own counsel, rarely sharing his reasons for allowing things to happen. Would it matter if he did? Would my heart ache any less if I knew why my son was killed? No. He would still be dead, and my heart would still be broken.

"How long, O Lord?" I whispered to the wall. "When will you deliver us?"

Two Years Earlier

An Announcement

"I don't like you today," I grumbled as I pushed myself to a sitting position. "Do you laugh at me when you watch me move?" Some might consider that blasphemy, but I liked to think that Yahweh knew me well enough to know otherwise.

A fire raged in my lower back, and moving only made it worse. Days like this, I should surrender to my age and remain in bed, while my wife massaged my aches. But my wife was miles away, and I had an appointment with Yahweh.

Groaning, I pulled myself to my feet and shuffled outside, bracing myself against a wall as I walked. Why was I even here? Why, after decades of obscurity, had I been chosen? Yahweh is not cruel, so he did not choose me just to laugh at me. No, he was choosing to honor my decades of service. I should be grateful, but all I felt was pain.

"Is this how you reward us?" I asked him as I bathed. "Waiting until we are too old to enjoy the honor?": The warm water relaxed my stiff muscles and made moving easier, more or less. My joints still ached, as they did most days anymore, and I reached for my walking stick.

When had I become such an old man? Wasn't it only yesterday that I was winning footraces among the village youth; being yelled at by the gray-beards as we dodged them in the street? My own beard was gray now, and my step as slow and hesitant as a new baby learning to walk. I stand still when the village boys race by, trusting them to avoid me, using my stick to steady myself. My body trembles with the desire to join their game, but my head over-rules my heart, as it should.

I am no boy, to race madly through the streets. I am as old as the grandfathers, and as feeble. While my heart still has the fire of youth, my body betrays me with its aches and pains, its creaking knees and slower steps. I should retire, I thought, and stay home with my wife. Instead, here I was on rotation at the temple, ignoring the pains of age as I dressed for the most important day of my career.

Not every priest is chosen for this task, and I honestly never thought it would fall to me. Yes, I follow the law, but I also question the law-giver. His commands rule our days, so we should understand them with our deepest selves. This means questioning, and challenging.

It's hard, sometimes, to challenge the Most High. He is law-giver, creator of all we see and have. How dare I argue with him? Who am I to question him? But he answers my questions, or so it seems to me. Sometimes I hear his words to Job: *"Where were you when I started all this?"* And I interpret that as him saying it's not time for me to know the answers. Other times, I get a spark of insight, a flash of brilliance that lights a confused shadow and shows me just enough to guide me to the next question. The flashes reassure me; encourage me to keep asking without fear of divine retribution. After all, our own writings tell us that it is Yahweh's glory to hide things and ours to discover them.

The others argue with me - they say it is the King's glory to discover them, but I remind them that Yahweh never meant for kings to rule over us. He was our King -- is our King, no matter what Rome decrees. And today, I will be in his temple, lighting the holy incense.

Why me? I whispered to Yahweh in my mind. Who am I, to be chosen by you for this task? I am no one, just one of many sons of Aaron dedicated to your service. Had this honor fallen years ago, I might have become someone important, but with my failing health and Elizabeth's sorrows, I had considered stepping down. So why now?

I knew there were others better suited for this honor - more respectful of Yahweh's priesthood. You should have seen their faces when the lot fell to me. For that matter, I wish I could have seen my own face. I had long since stopped thinking the lots would ever choose me. The elders would never select an argumentative old man, but apparently Yahweh would.

"Make me your servant, Yahweh," I murmured as I did every morning. *"Show me your ways, and set my feet in your paths, that I might not sin against you."*

*****

Taking several deep breaths to calm myself, I entered the Temple. It was an easy task to light the incense. The smoke billowed from it, more than incense should produce; and I stepped back coughing slightly, rubbing the sudden tears from my stinging eyes. Had I done something wrong? Was there a fire? But the incense was smoking normally now. The room brightened as the unusual smoke cleared and kept getting brighter, the light stinging my eyes as much as the smoke had. I blinked several times, trying to ease the stinging. The brightness was unbearable, far worse than looking at the noonday sun.

Unable to stand against the light, I fell to my knees and prostrated myself before the altar. "Most High Yahweh," I prayed. "If it is my time to die, I thank you that it is here, in your presence." But I did not die, and the light dimmed, damping its power as I might damp a lamp by covering it. I started to rise and stopped when I realized I was not alone. The light focused itself on the right side of the altar, glowing like flaming gold. I shielded my eyes with my hand, trying to see past the brightness to whatever was there. I knew it was not the Shekinah Glory or I would be dead already, my eyes burned out of their sockets by a chance glimpse of the one true god. But what was it? Not human, certainly, although it looked like a man, if there could be such a thing as a man made of pure light, fire dancing through and around him, covering him like a robe.

I prostrated myself again, swallowing hard to keep from spewing the bile rising in my throat.

Music filled my mind, calming my fear; singing to me of the wonder of creation; the majesty of El Shaddai; the joy in his original garden. A somber note intruded, and I wept for Adam's fall, his expulsion from the paradise our Lord had created for him. My heart ached as I watched Cain slay Abel; saw the flood ravaging the land. My peoples' history flashed before me as the music lifted and swelled; its notes filled with promise of joy and laughter, of the blessings so long denied my wife and me.

The vision faded, leaving me longing for more. I wanted to be back in the music, seeing again the impossible sight of my Elizabeth heavy with child, then holding our newborn son. But the music was over. The man of fire -- an angel, I realized suddenly -- was still there, waiting for my response.

"Can this really be true?" I wondered. "Can Yahweh really intend to provide us a son? We're too old! "

The angel flamed white-hot, although I had said nothing out loud.

"I am Gabriel! I stand in the presence of the Most High, and He sent me to deliver His message. You recognized me as His messenger, and yet you doubt His message? Hear me then. You will have no voice until what I proclaim has come to pass. Yes, your barren wife will conceive, and bear you a son, whom you shall name John. The Most High will fill him with His own presence, even as early as his birth, and you will raise him according to the decrees I now give you."

He continued speaking, giving me instructions, and my scholar's mind absorbed and remembered them, even as I wept in joy. A final blaze of brightness and the room was empty again, save for the altar. Stumbling a little, I left the temple, surprised to see the other priests crowded near the entrance.

"What happened?"

"Why were you so long?"

"Could you not see the light out here?" I asked them, but no sound left my throat.

A Moment of Wonder

Hear me, Brothers! Gather round and share this marvel.

You know me: like you, I am a messenger of the One True God. Created before time began, I spend my life in His presence, attending to His every word, doing His bidding to accomplish His will.

With you, I built a staircase of stars so Jacob could see Yahweh's messengers traveling to and from Earth. I was there to hear Sarah laugh when Yahweh told her husband she would bear a son. I met Hagar in the desert, guiding her and Ishmael to an oasis. I stood at the door with you, and listened to Egypt's lamentations the night her children died.

For centuries, I have watched Yahweh's chosen people alternately follow and reject Him. For centuries, I have watched the Most High as He watched them, and marveled at His restraint. How He can love such a stiff-necked people is beyond me. But love them He does, interfering only when necessary.

From the time I was created, I have observed them; sometimes from a distance, sometimes face to face. But never have I seen what I saw today; the absolute trust in her heart, the complete confidence in her mind.

I am *Gabriel*!

Yahweh allows me to see the hearts of those to whom I bring His messages. Always, there is fear, hesitation, and doubt. Once I am recognized, they tremble, sometimes falling on knees that no longer support their weight. But not today. Today, I witnessed a marvel such as I have not seen since Adam first walked in Eden.

This young girl, barely a woman -- what faith she has! I met her, blazing with the glory of the One True God, and though she recognized me, she did not panic. When she heard Yahweh's words, her only concern was for His success.

Her life will be changed in ways she cannot imagine. Her faith will be tested as Job's, and her only concern is that Yahweh's plan succeeds. I know my creator is infallible, able to know all things, see all things, and do all things. Even so, I am marveling today at His unerring wisdom in choosing this almost-child to fulfill His plan.

All glory truly belongs to Him who created all things, and who will not rest until His people are reconciled to Him.

A Choice

The angel disappeared as quickly as he had come, leaving me trying to absorb the message I had just heard. Had he really said that Yahweh wanted *me* to bear our Deliverer? I was no one, from a nowhere town. But the angel was real, blazing flame without catching the straw on fire.

"Is that what Moshe's burning bush had been like?" I wondered, then shook my head. I could ponder that later, when I had time to dream. Right now, I needed to tell Joseph -- Joseph!

Would he believe me? Of course he would. He knows me, and he knows Yahweh. We would have to get married sooner than we had planned. Oh, I should tell my parents, too. Maybe I should tell them first. It was almost meal time; we could talk after we'd eaten.

I had to force myself to eat. I wanted to dance around the room, bouncing from wall to wall, from ceiling to floor.

"Mama, can we wait to clean up? I need to tell you something."

"You cannot talk and work?"

"Not for this. I promise, I'll clean up as soon as we're done. No, Papa - don't leave. I need to tell both of you."

They exchanged glances, and I could almost hear them thinking they should humor their dreamer. Mama started stacking the dishes.

"Mama!" I protested.

"Talk is easier over a clean table," she insisted. "Come now, it won't take long."

She was right of course, but in my impatience, it felt like forever. Finally, we sat down again. Or they did. I could not sit still; could not stop smiling.

"Tell us then," Papa said. "What has put the stars in your eyes today? A special dream, perhaps?" He chuckled, but I answered him soberly.

"No dream, Papa. Not this time. Just plain old good news. I'm going to have a baby!"

His chair crashed behind him as he stood.

"What!?!? How dare he? Where is that carpenter? Why isn't he here with you confessing this sin?"

Mama said nothing, staring at her hands, tracing an old scar with her fingers. Papa's words suddenly sank in.

"What? No, Papa -- calm down. It's not Joseph! He is an honorable man, you know that. He would never do something like that."

This did not calm him like I thought it would.

"Then who -- how --" he stopped speaking, breathing heavily, clenching and unclenching his fists. Mama took over.

"Mary...listen to your words, and think of what you are saying. You, a betrothed woman, are pregnant. And Joseph is *not* the father? Why do you say this is good news? Do you not want to marry him?"

I laughed. "Of course I do! I cannot even imagine being with anyone but him."

"But you *were*!" Papa groaned through his hands. He wouldn't look at me.

"I what?" It was my turn to be confused. "No, I haven't been with anyone else. I wouldn't break my vows to Joseph."

"Did you dream this, then? Some dreams seem as real as day."

"It was no dream," I answered Mama. "He was as real as you are, asking for my help. How could I say no?"

"MARY!" Papa's bellow was usually reserved for crowds. "What happened? Start at the beginning."

"I was in the stable, feeding our donkey, and suddenly he was there, saying he had a message for me. Honestly, I thought he was lost, and meant some other Mary, but he assured me I was the one. So we talked --"

"WHO?" Papa bellowed again. "Tell me who dishonored my little lamb."

"No one, Papa. I am not dishonored. I am blessed. That's how he said it. *Blessed are you, more than all the other women in the world, for you have been chosen-*"

"Chosen." Papa interrupted again. "Chosen for what?"

"To have this baby." I was getting frustrated. "Weren't you listening?"

Papa groaned again.

"Mary." Mama sounded as old as her own mother, just then. "Sit down and start over. Help us to understand this.

"You were in the stable feeding our donkey, and then --"

"And then *he* showed up, and called me blessed!"

"And told you to have his baby?"

"Not *his* baby - Yahweh's!" I was moving again, unable to

keep still. "Yahweh chose *me* to have his baby!" I paused, but neither of them spoke. Papa was groaning again, and Mama's hand was at her heart, as if it pained her.

"The angel said --"

"Angel!?!?" Papa roared. "This man told you he was an ANGEL!?!?!?!"

"Papa, please...He *was* an angel, on fire with Yahweh's power -"

"You lit a fire in our stable? The STABLE?"

"Joachim, hush." Mama stroked his arm. "Describe this angel, Daughter, so we can be sure."

"He was all light, Mama, so bright that I could see the spilled grain in the corners. The dust sparkled like diamonds in his glow. I couldn't even look at him, and had to close my eyes.

"He called my name, and it sounded like you sounded when I was sick that one time, all caring and concerned. *Don't be scared,* he said, but I wasn't scared; it was just too bright. Even through my closed eyes I could see how bright he was. Then it wasn't as bright, and I could open my eyes again.

"Do you remember the fire in the grove, and how the flames chased each other from one tree to the next? He looked like that somehow, but at the same time, he looked like gold that had been melted, kind of flowing over and around and through everything.

"His eyes were diamond-sharp and crystal clear. But when he looked at me they changed, and reminded me of a summer sky. He smiled at me then, and told me I was chosen out of all the women who were ever born, to fulfill Yahweh's plan for our Deliverer.

"What was I supposed to do, Papa? I couldn't say no. I thought he had the wrong Mary. I reminded him that I am still untouched, but he told me that when Yahweh wants something to happen, it happens. OH! Mama -- you'll never guess! He said Elizabeth is pregnant, too!"

"Elizabeth?" Mama repeated. "*Our* Elizabeth? She's too old!"

"He said that, too. It was when he was telling me that Yahweh can do anything. He said she's in her sixth month already"

"What does this mean, 'Achim?" Mama almost whispered her question to Papa, but we both heard her. He covered her trembling hands with his, then released her long enough to pull me into his embrace.

"What does it mean?" He repeated. "It means we're going to have a baby."

We stayed like that, Mama and I on either side of Papa, leaning into his strength and thinking private thoughts, until I thought of my beloved.

"I have to tell Joseph!" I started to pull away, but Papa held me.

"Wait, Daughter. We must consider this."

"But he needs to know! We need to move the wedding date, and --"

Papa shushed me with his finger on my lips. "Hush, child. Your mother and I need to talk. There's plenty of time yet to tell your carpenter."

As I lay in bed that night, I imagined that I could already feel my body changing. I knew I was being silly, but I couldn't help myself. I couldn't wait to tell Joseph, smiling as I pictured his excitement at the news. When I remembered my parents' reaction, the smile fled. They hadn't really believed me at first. Would he? I tried to reassure myself, but the doubt was there now, nibbling away at the joy I had felt since meeting the angel.

"Yahweh, help me do this for you," I whispered. "Don't let me fail you. You have honored me beyond all others - help me be worthy of such honor."

I could hear the low murmur of my parents' voices, and it soothed me to sleep.

A Miracle

There were days when all I could do was rest on the unchanging truth that is our Lord. *"Hear, O Israel, Yahweh is our God. Yahweh is one God."* It didn't answer my questions, but it reminded me that Yahweh is who he is, and does what he does. He is not a carved piece of wood or stone, whose actions could be manipulated by man -- he is the Holy One of Israel, who brought us out of bondage and into our promised land. Who was I to argue with his decisions? So I didn't argue, but that doesn't mean I didn't hurt.

Nights were the worst times. Daytime was busy time, filled with all the activity of life. But at night, I would stare at the ceiling listening to Zach's snores, and wonder what I had done wrong.

"Children are the heritage of the Lord," but not for me. *"He will give you the desires of your heart,"* but he didn't. Yahweh is perfect, so the fault must be mine, but I couldn't figure out what I had done to deserve this punishment.

"Show me my sin," I begged our creator, "so I can repent." I listened to the rabbis, followed the commandments as best I could, but nothing ever changed. Each month, I watched the moon's path across the sky, from waxing to waning to waxing again, hoping this would be the month my shame ended. But each month was the same, as my body's flow crushed my hopes. Zach would hold me while I cried, stroking my hair but having no way to ease my heart.

In the morning chill, I would wash all traces of tears from my face, bury my heart-pain under a smile for the sunrise, and face the day, and my friends' pity. Of course I knew they pitied me; how could they hide it? Conversations would stop mid-sentence when I entered a room, sidelong glances trying to gauge how much I had heard. And the advice they gave!

Sometimes I felt like Job, beset on all sides by friends who thought they knew best when they really knew nothing at all. I should drink this special tea at a certain time each month, and I would conceive. Or I should stop hiding my secret sin; confess all to Yahweh, and his forgiveness on the Day of Atonement would lift the curse that blocked my womb. Truly, if I knew about a secret sin, I would have confessed it a hundred times over. I fail my Lord on a daily basis: none of us can keep his laws, not even the High Priest, but *he* has a house full of children.

Remembering Sarah and Hannah, I never stopped asking for the blessing Yahweh promised all women. His ways are not our ways after all, and his thoughts are higher than our thoughts. That's how I answered the advice-givers, and they praised me for my faith even as they shook their heads at my words. One day, I'd had enough. Enough of my two-faced friends, enough of my creator's silence, enough of the shame that dogged my days. It was more than I could bear, and I retreated to our room. Zach found me curled into myself on our bed, eyes red and swollen from tears. He sat beside me, lifted my head and placed it in his lap, started stroking my hair. He didn't ask what was wrong - he knew.

"We'll keep trying," he said, as he'd said every month, but I shook my head and pushed myself off the bed, turning away from him.

"No." My voice was rough, harsh with disappointment. I swallowed, blinking back tears, and faced him again, caressing his cheek. "No, Zach. It has been ten years already. If Yahweh wanted us to have children, we would." I paused, digging for the courage I needed for what I would say next. "If you want a different wife, one who's not defective, I'll --"

"Defective!?!?" He almost shouted the word, startling me. "You are *not* defective! Yahweh may keep children away from us, but as long as you are here, life is good." His fingers closed around my hand, pulling me onto his lap, into the shelter of his arms.

"You are my wife, and that is enough for me." He kissed the top of my head as I leaned into him. "You are my wife," he repeated. "Yahweh gave you to me, and I will not throw away his gift."

I wept again, but this time the tears were peaceful, strange though that may sound. His words had released a knot of fear constricting my heart. I hadn't known it was there until it was gone. He would not divorce me and marry another in the hopes of gaining a family. We would be our own family; Yahweh, Zach, and me. Comforted by this assurance, I lay back down, resting my head in his lap and listening to him speak my own thoughts out loud.

"We'll be our own family," he said softly. " Yahweh, you, and me. It is enough, Elizabeth. It is enough, and then some." But I did not hear that last bit. I was already asleep.

The birds woke me, their morning songs spreading cheer that out-ran the rising sun. I eased out of bed, trying not to disturb Zach. When he came to breakfast, he stopped in the doorway, staring. I laughed at the look on his face: my plan to surprise him had worked.

"Come! Eat before it grows cold," I chided him, still giggling.

"What?" It was not often my priest found himself at a loss for words, but he truly was.

"Hush." I placed my finger over his lips. "Did you not say we would be our own family?"

"Yes, but... What's all this?" His gesture encompassed the entire room, the table groaning with food, and me in my best gown.

"This is our new beginning." I smiled at him, knowing my smile was as free and joyful as on our first morning together. He smiled too, the memory of that first morning sparkling in his eyes. I filled our plates, then sat beside him as I had done all those years ago.

"Good morning, husband." Thus had I greeted him on our wedding morn, and I knew he remembered.

"Good morning, wife," he replied, reaching for my hand just as he had done then.

That was indeed our new beginning, so long ago that I rarely remembered the dark days that came before it. We made a good family, and Zach was right; it was more than enough. There were still times I had to resist being jealous of a new mother, but Yahweh never failed us, and he filled our hearts and our home with his people. As the years passed, acceptance became contentment. We had a good life - a very good life. Then Yahweh shone his favor upon us, selecting Zach to be the priest who lit the incense, and our world turned upside down.

I am an old woman now, well past the age of motherhood. And yet I am a mother; our son grows inside me, and each day I see new changes proving this truth. Well, the changes prove that *something* is growing inside me, but whether it is life or death is too soon to tell. Zach says life; Yahweh's Messenger told him we would have a son. Zach says his muteness is the proof of this - the Messenger took his voice and it will not return until our son is born. I believe him, but I'm not sure our friends do. Yes, those very same friends who urged me to confess my non-existent secret sin are now wondering if Yahweh's Messenger really said what Zach claims he said. They think he simply lost his voice from shock at seeing the Messenger.

When they think I can't hear them, they speak of senility and illness, even delusions. I ignore their whispers as I ignored their long ago advice, but sometimes at night, I wonder. Some nights I lie awake as Zach snores beside me, wishing the Messenger could have muted that too, staring at the ceiling, and remembering crushed dreams. It is during those nights I am most grateful for Yahweh's unchanging nature.

The God of our Fathers is not a prankster, like some gods other people follow. He is not spiteful and does not play tricks for cheap laughs. He is the one true God, who made Abraham a great nation; who guided Moshe as he led us out of Egypt; who anointed a young shepherd and made him our greatest king. He told Zach we're having a son, and that means it is life growing inside me, not some killing illness.

Those are my middle-of-night conversations with myself. Most times they reassure me, but some nights I leave the comfort of my husband's arms and pace on our roof, searching the night sky for my own messenger from Yahweh, trying not to hate myself for my doubts.

I may have never had a child, but I know the stages. The mornings when nothing stays in your stomach - I've experienced those. The days when everything beautiful moves you to tears - I've had those, too. Poor Zach: he was so confused on the day he found me weeping as I watched a storm move across the desert. I wasn't hurt, nor worried about the storm; just awed by the power of our creator who could bring a storm from a cloudless sky.

"It's the baby," I told him as I dried my tears. "All mothers go through this." My visiting friends nodded agreement, each pausing to reassure him as they left.

Jerusha started to leave, but came back to sit by me after talking to him. "He worries, Elizabeth." She patted my hand. "So do we, a little. At your age, with no other babies..." She left her next thought unspoken, but I answered it anyway.

"Yes, we are certain it is a baby. You know the ways a woman changes; I see those changes in myself. And Yahweh's messenger cannot lie. Besides," and I watched her closely as I made my strongest argument "I have felt the flutters of his movement."

She patted my hand again, making me wish it would not be rude to just snatch it away. "I'm sure you felt something my dear, but are you certain it wasn't just indigestion?"

Now I did snatch my hand away. "Jerusha! We are *not* delusional!"

She nodded, but would not meet my eyes. "We fear for you, my sister," she finally said. "You know that there have been women who wanted children so much that their bodies began --"

I interrupted her blasphemy. "Jerusha, listen to me, and tell the others. There *was* a messenger from Yahweh. Zacharias saw him clearly. Our son grows inside me, and when he is born, you will know your concerns were unfounded. We will not speak of this again."

She started to speak, but I was firm. "This discussion is over."

Her lips pressed into a thin line and her cheeks flushed. At last she sighed deeply, patted my hand, and said "You know best, I suppose."

I smiled at her. "Sometimes I'm convinced I know nothing, but Yahweh knows best, and I trust him."

"I hope you're right," she said, rising again to leave. "I sincerely hope you're right."

"So do I," but those words were only in my mind, where she could not hear them.

That night, my doubts overwhelmed my reason. Unable to sleep, I left my snoring husband and climbed the steps to our roof, seeking solace in the night sky. The stars reminded me of Yahweh's promise to Abraham, and my mind bounced from one promise to another. Abraham, Isaac, Jacob, Joseph, Moshe, David, Daniel...our God has always been faithful to his people, even when we were unfaithful. Leaning on the wall, I rested my hands on the bulge that was my son, and prayed.

"You are the God of our fathers, the God of our family, creator of our world, and of this life growing inside me. I know this, Yahweh, as surely as I know the sun will rise tomorrow. Why, then, do I give any credence to her harping? Yes, I know why; because of the barren years, before you gave me peace. I need your peace now, Lord...defend me from my enemies; strengthen my heart so I may rest in you.

"There *is* life growing inside me, a son we shall name John. He will be your servant, our gift to you in exchange for your gift to us." I stopped speaking, but my thoughts argued with my prayer, whispering *"What if?"*. I saw a barren field in my mind, wheat stalks scorched by desert sun, vineyards parched for lack of water. What if this baby *was* senile delusion, and the barren fields the reality?

"Even so, Lord," I spoke again. "Whether this be delusion or reality, you are my creator, God of my fathers and of my family. You, Zach & I have been family for more than half my life. It is enough -- no, it is more than enough. I believe what your Messenger said, but if we find that Zach was mistaken in what he heard, it doesn't matter. You are my God, and my deepest desire is for your glory."

I had no more words to speak, and no more fears disturbed my thoughts. I opened eyes I hadn't realized were closed, and saw Zach in front of me, wiping away tears. He stood beside me and I slipped inside the curve of his open arm, leaning my head on his shoulder. He laid his other hand beside mine on the bulge that was our son, and rested his cheek on the top of my head as we watched the stars give way to morning.

An Argument

"Tears?" I laughed at her, hating myself for doing it, but also feeling a perverse joy as she flinched from it.

"Are those supposed to make me less angry, make me feel sorry for you instead of feeling betrayed?"

She just sat there with her eyes closed, not answering. I clenched and unclenched my fists, trying to calm myself.

"Tell me something believable," I pleaded with her. "Tell me he forced you, and I'll defend your honor. But don't blaspheme. And don't lie to me. You're not a good liar."

I paused, giving her a chance to redeem herself, to justify her betrayal, but she still said nothing.

I glanced at her, but looked away quickly. I was glad I couldn't see her eyes. Her head was down, so I didn't know if they were still closed, but I could see her tears splash off her clenched fists.

I sighed. Her tears were almost enough to stop my anger, but her story was too ridiculous to be true.

"Fine." I almost growled at her. "Silence is better anyway. I need to think."

I turned away from her, but turned back when she made a noise. I thought she was finally ready to tell me the truth, but she still wasn't talking. Instead, she had wrapped her arms around herself and given in to the tears. The noise I'd heard was a sob, muffled because she had pressed her mouth against her arm.

I sighed again, and walked back to her, almost lifting her off the rock. She snuggled into my embrace like a lost lamb, still sobbing. I stroked her hair and made soothing noises. She was finally talking, but I could barely hear her. I bent my head until it rested on hers.

"I'm sorry, I'm sorry, I'm sorry..." she kept repeating it, and my heart lifted. Maybe now she'd confess her sin.

"Tell me, Mary." I almost whispered the words. "What really happened? Whose baby is this?"

She stiffened, and took a deep breath.

"Yahweh has honored me above all other women," she replied, just as she had said at first. "He has chosen me --"

She stopped as I finished her sentence for her. "To bear his Deliverer. Yes, you said that already. I thought you were ready to tell me the truth!"

"Joseph, it *is* the truth. Please believe me. I would never lie to you."

"Blasphemer!" I was angry again; wouldn't any man be? "You break our vows and then blame it on God. I thought I knew you. I thought you were an honorable woman. Apparently, I was wrong on both points."

I walked away without looking back, not wanting to see her face, not caring whether she followed me.

When I reached my shop, I flung the door open, enjoying the sound of it slamming against the wall. My workshop has always been my haven. This is where I retreat when the world makes no sense. A few hours spent joining wood together brings the world back into balance for me. But not today. I picked up a piece of wood but it felt like a club, and I dropped it before I destroyed all my projects.

I was surrounded by my broken dreams. The marriage bed I was making, with the carvings. How many nights had I spent on that, working after the shop was closed, pouring all my hopes into it? The work table, tailored to her height so she would not exhaust herself in the kitchen. The plates, bowls, eating utensils; I was so happy to be making new things for the house to celebrate our new lives with each other. And now...they might as well be firewood. I would get no use of them now, and couldn't bear the thought of selling them to someone else.

My world had shattered, and I could see no way to fix it. There was no pattern to this, like there is in my projects. This was chaos invading my mind, poisoning my thoughts, driving me crazy. I would find no peace in my workshop today. I left, the door swinging behind me, not even checking to see if it fully closed.

Anger and confusion ruled my thoughts, coupled with the need to flee, to hide like a wounded animal. My steps pulled me away from town into the hills. Suddenly, I realized where I was heading. This was the same route I had walked earlier with my betrothed, the same path that led to "our place." We had a quiet spot in the low hills where we would sit and talk, hidden from the world. It had always been a place of peace for me, like my workshop; but like my workshop, I would find no peace there today.

It was in that peaceful haven my world ended. It was there my betrothed confessed her infidelity.

How *could* she!?

How *dare* she?!

And then to lie to me, to blaspheme like she did. I shook my head, frowning. I would never have expected that from her. But then, I would never have expected her infidelity, either. Sighing, I sat down on "our" rock. The desert sky was melting into a rainbow, holding the darkness at bay for a while yet, but nothing could stop the darkness already entering my heart. She had betrayed me. So had Yahweh.

How could I ever trust anyone again? A star twinkled above the rainbow sky, winking at me.

"Easy for you," I thought at it. "Your world hasn't ended." It brightened as if to cheer me, but I was beyond cheering.

I was stupid to come here: there were too many memories, too many dreams in this place. I walked over to the stack of pebbles where I had planned the eventual expansion of my shop and stared at it, remembering her joy at my excitement. I kicked it apart, pebbles scattering. Stooping, I collected a handful and threw them, one by one, as far as I could, wishing I could tie my pain to each one, and toss it away too.

"I **trusted** you!" I shouted at the Most High. "You said she was the one, didn't you? Then why did you let this happen? I can't marry her now; not after this."

There were no more pebbles to throw, no more stones to kick. Grown men don't cry, but my face and beard were wet. Slowly, my clenched fists opened. I sat again on our rock, where she had sat only hours before, holding back her tears. Mary almost never cries. She isn't one of those women who uses tears to get her way. Yet I accused her of that. In the throes of my own pain, I wanted to cause her pain, so I hit her with my words and my disbelief. I would take back my words if I could, but that wouldn't make her story any more believable.

It couldn't really be true, could it? Would Yahweh do such a thing? Yes, he would send a deliverer as he promised, but from *Nazareth*? I love my town, but we hardly qualify as a place to birth a deliverer.

My anger was gone, washed away by my tears. All that remained was the pain and dry dust of shattered dreams. I sat on our rock, my heart as empty as a dry well, and waited for Yahweh to fill it again.

"Yahweh," I whispered. "Help me understand. Show me your way, and give me the courage to follow. "

The sky faded from orange to black, the twinkling stars trying to coax a smile from me, but I had no more smiles. I wasn't sure I would ever smile again. Mary was my smile, the song that filled my heart, and she was lost to me now as completely as if she were dead.

Did I hear Yahweh wrong? Was she *my* choice and not his? But I knew that wasn't true. As surely as Yahweh meant for Isaac to be with Rebekah, he meant me to be with Mary.

"Tell me what to do Yahweh," I begged. I couldn't think clearly. Should I go through with this, and raise another man's child as my own? Would I be a fool? What would people say – but do I care what people would say?

"What will happen if I put her away? Will they stone her?" The night sky dimmed at that thought, fast-moving clouds hiding the stars.

Yahweh stayed silent, as I expected. This was my problem, not his. Unless what she said was true. But it couldn't be true, could it?

I stood up, then prostrated myself before our rock as if it were an altar.

"You are El Shaddai, Jehovah Shammah, God of my ancestors and of my life. Show me your way, and help me walk in it. Your law says to put her away, to punish her sins. I will do that if you tell me to, but I really don't want to. Show me, Yahweh...I am lost in the darkness of sorrow and need your light to find my way."

*****

He was so angry. I was frightened, even though I was confident he would not hit me. My Joseph is not a violent man. We had been sitting on our rock, in our quiet place. I love that hidden clearing, the view of town below us and the desert stretching beyond our fields and flocks. I could not even see it today; all I saw was my broken heart as Joseph unleashed his anger. He did not yell at me: I wish he had, because I could have gotten angry in return. But his voice was quiet, which made his words even harsher.

"*Yahweh* gave you a child? I'm supposed to believe that? You're lucky he doesn't strike you right where you sit, blaspheming like that. I have to admit, it's the most inventive excuse I've ever heard for cheating."

He pitched his voice to falsetto: "I had to say yes -- it was God himself asking me!" Back to his normal baritone. "Mary, just tell me who it was. Tell me he forced you -- I'll believe you, and defend your honor with my life. But if you can't trust me with the truth..." his voice trailed off.

I did not answer him. I could not; I had no words to defuse his wrath. My jaw ached from locking my sobs behind my clenched teeth, but I could not lock the tears behind my eyes. They leaked through my closed eyelids, and when he saw them, he grew angrier.

"And now you play with tears," he said, "thinking to soften my heart. You're not the woman I thought I knew, and I don't want to know this crazy woman you've become."

He left me there, his robe billowing from the breeze he created, dust rising and settling in his wake. I stayed, unable to move, to think; un-nerved by his unexpected reaction. Did he just end our betrothal? Was I doomed to a reputation as a loose woman, with a son all would consider illegitimate? My hands cradled my stomach, instinctively protecting the child who was still too small to be visible, but who was assuredly growing inside me.

He didn't believe me. How could he think I would lie to him? I know it sounds crazy, but I also know it's true. I remembered Elizabeth telling me how John leapt in joy, and heard again the wonder in her voice: "*Who am I, that the mother of our Lord should come to me?*"

I did not dream this, or lie to cover a night's foolishness. This was Yahweh, no matter what Joseph thinks, and how could I say "no" to my Lord? I remembered my answer to the Angel: "*Yahweh is my Lord -- he can do whatever he wants with me.*" Did I still mean that? Would I say it again if he were here now, even if Joseph never believed me?

Yahweh is the Lord of my life, the God of my ancestors and my heart. What he asks of me, I will do, even if it costs my life. And if I will trust him with my life, I will also trust him with my reputation. I was not forced. It was no human who placed this child within me. He is Yahweh's son, and Yahweh will protect us.

"Yahweh, I know I should trust you more – I truly believe this is your doing. But I cannot help worrying about what Joseph will decide. I hope he will change his mind, realize I would never lie to him. But even if he doesn't, you will provide.

"Help me trust you," I whispered as I wiped the last of my tears away. "I am your handmaiden still – have your way in my life."

A Prayer

When I was young, I cut my hand helping prepare dinner. I remember staring at the cut, watching the blood welling out of it, dripping onto the table, and felt no pain until my mother's voice penetrated my shock. Then the pain was almost unbearable, and I screamed out to her for help. She tended my hurt as mothers do, and I was soon fine, although the cut left a scar. I looked at it now, tracing its edges with my fingers, wishing Mama were still here and that this pain could heal as easily as a simple cut.

My little girl is having a baby. This should be the most joyous news a mother could hear, but I had little joy in my heart. When she was a child, I could protect her from heartache. Now she is grown, and her heart is breaking.

I moved around the house, dusting shelves that showed no dust, tidying things that were perfectly tidy. But I saw none of it. All I could see were the tears in my daughter's eyes when she came back from walking with Joseph. Just as I had feared, he did not believe her.

Could I blame him? Her story was impossible; the only reason I believed her is because my Mary has never lied to me. And she was right about Elizabeth; my aged cousin is now the proud mother of a son. Only Yahweh could make that happen, and if he could do that, he could give my baby a child. And she is definitely expecting a child. Before long, the villagers will notice, and tongues start to wag. The gossips would love a story like this, and act as if it had never happened before. They would cackle about how first babies can come anytime, while all the others take nine months.

Usually, it just means embarrassment for the couple; an acknowledgement that nothing is secret in a village. Usually, it just means that that wedding will be sooner than planned. But not for my Mary. This baby could mean her death.

I stumbled, and the room darkened around me. I fumbled for the nearest chair, almost dropping into it. My little girl could die, and there's nothing I could do to stop it.

"Yahweh," I whispered, pressing my hands against my eyes, trying to block the tears burning my eyelids. "Can you help us? *Will* you help us? If it is truly your child...what am I saying? Of course it is yours. Our Mary doesn't lie, and while she may be a dreamer, she would not dream *that*. Forgive me, Lord, but follow my thoughts, if you don't mind.

"Your messenger told Mary to have your baby, and she agreed. But what about Joseph? If he doesn't believe her, if he names her adulteress, she will die, and your deliverer with her.

"Is that really your plan? I know your ways are not our ways, but I can't understand that type of plan at all. "

The sound of the door interrupted my thoughts.

"Joachim? Were you successful?"

Joachim walked into the room, and my tears started again. He is a big man, strong and capable, but tonight, with his shoulders slumped and his head downcast, I could see that his hair was mostly gray. Joachim was getting old: I had not noticed that before.

"He wouldn't listen?" I choked on the question, willing myself not to cry again.

"He wasn't there. The shop door was open, but all the rooms were empty, and he did not answer when I called his name."

"So you didn't talk to him?"

"Did I not just say he wasn't there?" He sighed. "I'm sorry, love. I'll try again in the morning."

"I'm scared, 'Achim." I almost whispered the words, but he heard me, and crossed the room to stand in front of me, pulling me off the chair and into his embrace. I leaned into him, his robe rough against my cheek. His arms tightened around me, strong and tender at the same time.

"So am I, love."

"What can we do? I'm her mother; I should be able to fix this, to make everything better."

His cheek was resting on the top of my head: I felt his jaw move as he answered. "She is a grown woman now, not a little girl. There's nothing we can do: it's between her and Joseph."

"And Yahweh. He's part of this too."

"And Yahweh," he agreed. "We can pray, and we can trust Yahweh's plan."

"I wish we knew his plan." That was as close to blasphemy as I would allow myself -- I couldn't admit that I wasn't sure Yahweh had a plan.

"We do know it; we just don't understand it."

I turned to look at him, our noses almost touching. His eyes were swollen and bloodshot; he had been weeping, too. He answered before I could ask.

"Of course we do. We know Yahweh plans to send us a

deliverer; we know he intends for Zacharias and Elizabeth to be parents; we know Yahweh has plans for each of us, whether we understand them or not."

"But do his plans for Mary include her death?"

"We all die, Anna...but not this young, and not by stoning." He sighed again. "I don't know his plans for her, or for Joseph, but I know they exist."

"But what if --"

"Hush, Love." His hand blocked my lips, stopping the next stream of worry. "We can bury ourselves in what-ifs, and have none of them come true. We must trust Yahweh."

Sometimes Joachim was too practical for me. I didn't want him to be practical right now. I wanted him to worry with me, so I would not be alone in my fear. I leaned into him again, craving the comfort of his embrace.

"I don't know if I can." I felt his chest rise and fall; his sigh fluttered my hair the way a breeze would.

"I know,." His tone was the same he used when our children were scared or hurt. "But we must try."

"If I could just *understand*..." my voice trailed off. Yahweh owed us no explanations. I sagged, my strength suddenly gone. Joachim gathered me up like a small child, and carried me to our bed. We lay beside each other, but I don't know if either of us slept. I know I didn't.

My mind had only one thought: "*Yahweh, help.*" As rhythmic as wood chopping, my prayer repeated: "*Yahweh, help. Yahweh, help.*"

I heard a rooster welcome the dawn, but I had no answering welcome in my own heart. This was the day my baby might die. Joachim's arm was around my waist, keeping us close.

I rested my trembling hand on his, and continued my plea.

"*Yahweh, help. Yahweh, help. Yahweh, help.*" My imagination pictured running feet, a mob racing to capture our Mary before she could flee, and I sped my words to match the footfalls.

"*YahwehhelpYahwehhelpYahwehhelp.*" Faster still, each syllable matching the sounds of the rushing crowd I heard in my mind. Or *was* it in my mind?

"Joachim!" I jabbed him with my elbow. "They're coming for her. Do you hear them?"

We both heard the slap of sandals rapidly hitting the ground, the harsh breath of one who had been running a long distance.

"Please, Yahweh," I whispered. My face was wet with new tears. "Please...they are already here, calling her name, eager to punish her supposed sin."

The runners were closer, their voices louder. I wanted to hide, as if my avoidance could postpone this pain, but Joachim pulled me to my feet, his smile mocking my tears.

"*Listen*, Anna! Quiet your fears, and *listen!*"

I glared at him, not understanding. Then I heard what he had heard. It was no crowd rushing to our house; just the footfalls of one person, staggering now as he ran. And one voice, calling a beloved name.

"MARY! I'm sorry, Mary!"

A Journey

My parents walked with us, Papa and Joseph in front of Mama and me. Mama would start to speak, then press her lips together and rub her face. I said nothing as we walked: all my words had already been said. We were right, and they knew we were right, but it was still hard for them to accept. It was hard for me, too.

In my mind, I relived the last discussion we'd had about this trip. They had agreed with us, but then when it was time to leave, Mama changed her mind.

"Think, child!" Mama had pleaded with me. "You should not travel so far in your condition. What if --" she stopped, not wanting to ill-wish. "Achim, tell her she must stay with us!"

Poor Papa. I don't think he knew what to say. He looked at her, reaching out to clasp her hand in his. He sighed and started to speak, but she stopped him.

"Don't say it." Her voice was low, and it shook as her chin quivered. "Don't tell me that my little girl is grown up now."

"Anna," he almost whispered. "She is still our daughter, but-- " he gestured towards Joseph, who spoke then to spare my father.

"She's still your daughter, but she's also my wife. It's my job to protect her now. "

"By taking her away from us?" Mama's voice was almost a screech.

"Mother Anna," he said softly. "This baby must be born in Bethlehem: you know that. Yes, it is several days travel, but we are well ahead of Mary's time. I would never put Mary or her baby in danger. "

Mama sighed, knowing Joseph was right. We had discussed all the prophecies, and had agreed that the prophet left no room for doubt. "*Out of Bethlehem*," he said, so to Bethlehem we must go.

"I wish I could go with you," she said. We had discussed that too, as a family, and decided against it.

"We'll be fine, Mama." I assured her again, hoping it was true. "We'll be staying with Joseph's family, after all."

"I know." she sighed, then repeated: "I know. But I worry."

"You would not be my mama if you did not worry about me. But all my life, you have taught me that Yahweh is with us and will protect us. We believe that, and we will trust Him for this journey."

"At least you're traveling with a caravan, instead of on your own."

Joseph and I looked at each other, not needing words to agree that neither of us would tell her we would only be with the caravan for part of the way.

We ate the next evening meal with my family, then said our goodbyes. Mama seemed surprised at that. "Are you not stopping by in the morning before you leave?"

"Mama," I began, but Joseph answered at the same time. I let him explain; sometimes Mama hears better when I'm not the speaker.

"We leave before daybreak," he said. "They suggested we join them tonight, so we'd be ready."

It had been more like a command than a suggestion, but Mama didn't need to know that.

"But you can't!" she stammered. "I'm not ready..."

Papa placed his hand on her shoulder. She gripped it with her own. "We will never be ready to say goodbye," he said. "So now is as good a time as any."

He clapped Joseph on the shoulder. "Safe travels, Son, and may Yahweh bring you safely back to us."

Mama looked tiny and old, almost lost, the way she had looked when her mother died. She gripped Papa's hand so tightly I could see her knuckles whiten under the skin.

Joseph looked from her to me, then back at her. "Would you like to walk with us to the camp?"

"Thank you," Papa answered over Mama's tears.

We walked in silence to the caravan's campsite, Papa and Joseph leading the way, with Mama and I behind them. Mama would start to speak, then press her lips together and rub her face. What would it be like, I wondered, when my own child was grown and starting his own life? How would I feel then?

When we stopped at the edge of the camp, I turned to face my parents, memories flooding my heart. I owed them so much. They had taught me to fear Yahweh and keep his commands, and they had believed me about the baby even though it seemed incredible. I embraced Mama as we both started to weep.

"Yahweh watch over us as we're apart," she whispered.

"And bring us back together," I answered. It was our traditional travel prayer.

"From your mouth to his ears," she replied, wiping her eyes.

"Joseph," she paused to swallow, then took a deep breath. "Watch over her, son of my heart, as Yahweh watches over you."

She turned and walked quickly away, as if she were too busy to stay, but I saw her shoulders shaking. I rested my head against Papa's chest as he hugged me; felt more than heard his blessing, and then it was just me and Joseph. And Yahweh. More than ever in my life, I felt his presence, and knew he watched over us.

*****

We stood together at the edge of the path, looking at a small village surrounded by fields of tents.

"There it is," Joseph pointed. "My ancestors' home."

"Joseph, what are all those tents?"

"Probably people here for the census," he replied. I gasped, and he smiled at me. "I'm sure many of them have already registered, and the Romans are extremely organized. It will be ok."

"I'm glad we're staying with your family," I told him. He nodded agreement.

We walked through the crowded streets to Ezra's home. Joseph had told me about his cousin during our journey. Like most homes, Ezra's had a guestroom upstairs, and we could stay there, he said.

Ezra welcomed us with smiles and kisses, introducing us to his wife and children.

"Of course you must stay here!" he boomed at Joseph. "You are *family*!" For such a thin man, he had a very loud voice.

"Thank you, Cousin." Joseph replied. "I have to admit, we didn't expect to see so many people here."

"The census." Ezra nodded. "Everyone in Galilee is from Bethlehem, it seems. In fact, we have others staying here, too." He frowned.

"Joseph, we *do* have others staying, and they are in the guest room."

"Should we find an inn, then?"

"What inn?" Ezra was booming again. "We are *family*!. No! You will stay here. We will make room."

It was not what I expected, but when does Yahweh follow our ideas? Since the beginning, he has done things his own way, and left it to us to broaden our understanding of him, or just to trust him. His ways are not our ways, after all. We moved into the lower level of Ezra's home, sleeping on our travel beds. Most nights were warm enough to keep the animals outside, so we were not actually sleeping with them, thank goodness. As the weeks passed, I was increasingly grateful that I did not have to climb to the roof every night.

Joseph worked with a local builder, and I helped Ezra's wife Deborah, when she would allow it. Her children were grown, with their own children near-grown, and her stories of their childhood made me smile, and long for the day when I would hold my own son.

"It won't be long now," she said one day, watching me push myself up from the bench near the wall. I started to answer, then stiffened suddenly and gasped at the pain that stabbed my back. I reached for her hand, and she came beside me, her embrace both comforting and encouraging.

"See? It might even be today!"

I was suddenly scared, not sure I could do this, and wishing Mama were here. Before I could say any of that, I doubled over from a new pain, gasping for breath. Deborah nodded, smiling. How could she smile when I was in such pain?

The contraction eased, and I was able to walk, as long as she supported me. We paced the room, waiting for my son to be ready to join us. When contractions struck, we paused, and I clung to her until the pain eased enough for me to walk again. Suddenly Joseph was there, supporting me as we walked, murmuring reassurances. I didn't realized Deborah had left until she returned, bringing her daughters with her.

"It is almost time," she said. "Joseph, help her to her bed, and then join Ezra. You should not be here."

"NO." We said together. I continued: "I can't have Mama here, but I will not chase my husband away."

"She needs me," he said simply, and he was right. It wasn't proper; it wasn't seemly; it wasn't traditional, but I needed him there. I gripped his forearm with no concern for his safety, even though I had heard of laboring women breaking bones with their grip. He sat beside me, stroking my hair, praying for our safety, and reassuring me just with his presence.

I knew the others were there, but his was the only voice I heard, until I drowned it with my own, calling for Mama. How I wished she were here! Or the angel I saw that time -- seeing him would distract me from this incredible pain.

"Joseph!" I heard the fear in my voice, as did he.

"You can do this, Mary. Don't quit now." He held my hand between his two, comforting me with his strength. My carpenter, my husband...twice-blessed am I, to have him in my life, a man who recognizes and listens to the voice of Yahweh.

The pain ran through me like water through a dry stream-bed, and my world faded to nothing but the sound of Joseph's voice and my body's shuddering attempts to launch this new life into its new world. There were no more thoughts, no more fears; just Joseph's voice, and his hand in mine. A fire burned in my mind, flaming gold calling my name. I reached for it, trying to answer, and the flames faded to glowing starlight, as if all the stars were shining in one place at one time.

Joseph's voice reached through the star-glow, but I didn't understand his words. He was holding the stars, offering them to me as his gift of love. As he placed them in my arms, I heard a baby cry, and felt my new-born son searching for his first meal.

I couldn't help laughing. Yes, it tickled, but it was more of an emotional release. I almost couldn't believe it had really happened. It was all so very impossible, and yet my son -- Yahweh's son -- was nestled in my arms.

Joseph and I smiled at each other, and I realized we were smiling through tears.

Deborah called Ezra to make Joseph leave. "The hard part is done now," she told him. "Now we just cut the cord, wrap him securely, and wait." He looked at me, and I nodded.

"Go," I told him. "I'm fine." He looked uncertain, but let Ezra lead him out, almost walking into the doorway because he kept looking back at me. I was surprised to see it was dark outside; it had been just after breakfast when the pains began.

When everything was cleaned up, the men returned. One of Deborah's daughters brought me some broth.

"You must restore your strength," she told me. "Your son needs a healthy mama." She blinked back tears as she looked at little Yshua. "Amazing," she murmured.

Yshua was sleeping, snug in the wrapping cloths. Joseph laid a horse pad over the hay in the feed bin, and placed the baby there, using his own outer robe as a cover.

As I ate the broth, I watched Joseph. He kept staring at his hands, turning them this way and that, opening and closing them. It was as if he had never seen them before.

"Joseph?" I kept my voice soft, not wanting to startle him. He looked at me, and I was surprised to see he was crying again. "Joseph? Is anything wrong?"

"Right here," he murmured, flexing his fingers. "All the stars of Heaven, held between my fingers. The light dazzled my heart..." His voice trailed off as he examined his hands again.

"I'm a builder. I've held wood and stone, even fire. But stars? No one can hold the stars. No one can reach them."

"You did." Deborah's voice was as quiet as Joseph's. "Your hands glowed with starlight, brightening the entire room. It's still here. " She waved her arms, drawing our attention to the unlit lamps.

"I've never seen a room light itself; never seen a man hold the stars. Is it this baby, or the two of you?"

I took a deep breath, asking Yahweh to guide my words as I answered her, but someone started pounding on the door, so violently that it shook in its hinges. Loud voices called for someone to answer, to let them see the miracle.

Joseph rose, finally looking away from his hands. As he neared the door, Deborah retrieved Yshua from the manger, and gave him to me. I held him close, gaining courage from his nearness. Joseph opened the door, filling the frame with his body, silhouetted between the torchlight outside and the room-glow within.

"Let these be friends," I prayed, and was suddenly assaulted by the noise of a dozen or more men all talking together. They pushed their way inside, overwhelming Joseph. They were rough-dressed, faces pinched with cold, smelling of wood smoke and dung. A lamb maneuvered its way through their legs, and walked towards me, bleating softly. The men quieted at the sound, staring at me and my son; shuffling their feet and twisting their hands together.

"I'm sorry," one of them said to us, "but we had to see if it was true."

"True?" Joseph asked, moving beside me. I handed Yshua to him, and he put him back in his bed, covering him with his robe.

"A baby, sleeping in a feed bin, is what the angel said."

"Angel?" Joseph asked. "I'm sorry, I must sound stupid, but I have no idea what you're talking about."

They all started talking again, until a shrill whistle silenced them. In the quiet, we heard the lamb bleat again. He was on his hind feet, front feet resting on the edge of my son's bed; looking for hay, I supposed.

"I'm sorry, little lamb." I said. "We had to use the feed bin as a bed."

As if he understood me, the lamb dropped to all fours, then laid down beside the manger, drifting to sleep as the grizzled shepherd shared their story.

A Choir

"It should be windy," I thought. *"A night this cold should have a strong wind to explain its frostiness. Then again, it shouldn't be this cold, this time of year."* I blew on my hands, rubbing them together to bring the feeling back. It helped for a few seconds, but the bitter cold stole the feeling from my fingers, leaving only the memory of warmth.

"Cold and dark," I muttered. "Just like life. Dark and empty, freezing the hope out of a man's heart."

My rounds completed, I took my frozen hands and feet back to the fire and my companions there. Some nights, we would talk, but this night froze the words in our brains. We huddled near the flames, only moving to add more fuel. All too soon, it was time for rounds again. I stayed near the feeble warmth of the fire, grateful that some other fool would face the cold night this time.

Usually, I love my job. I like being away from the village and depending only on myself -- my wits, my strength, my skills -- and occasionally on my companions. I enjoy watching the sheep, thinking of our Shepherd-King David and the years when Yahweh's favor made our nation strong.

Even night-watches are enjoyable, most nights. We gather near the fire between our rounds, discussing weighty topics like which wood makes the best staff, who can sling a stone the farthest, and whether Yahweh would honor his promises to us. We always declared his faithfulness of course, but I have to admit that sometimes I wonder. It has been so long since the days of David and Solomon, and between Herod and the Romans, it seems all our glory is behind us.

But still Yahweh promised to send a Messiah to deliver us. He had delivered us before, sending Moshe to lead us from Egypt, and Nehemiah to bring us home from Babylon. Surely he would keep this promise too, and bring us another hero. Most nights, as I watched the stars move across the sky, I could believe Yahweh's promises. This was not most nights. This was a night to breed doubt and fear, not hope and faith.

Nights like this, I hate my job, and sometimes even my life. Oh, I know it's blasphemy to say that -- Yahweh gave me this life, and I should be grateful for it. But sometimes I wished for a different life, a life when we were still a proud nation rather than a conquered people.

Oppression steals the warmth from a man's soul the way this night's cold stole the warmth from my hands. Oppression blocks the light from a man's heart the way this night made the stars grow dim. My thoughts were disheartening and I glanced at the sky, expecting to see the stars prove me wrong, but no stars were twinkling.

I slowly closed my eyes and reopened them, telling myself the fire had momentarily blinded me. My second glance was the same as my first: there were no stars in the clear sky above me. I called the others and they stood with me, staring into the empty sky. Our night sky is never empty. The stars blaze above us, filling the sky with Yahweh's glory. Sometimes the moon glows as well, hanging low and full over the hillsides, or sharing a sliver of itself as it prepares for its next appearance. If no stars are visible, we see the clouds that hide them, and feel the storms or winds that come with the clouds. But not this night. There were no clouds, and no stars. The sky was clear, and as empty as our lives.

No matter how old I get, I will remember the way my stomach clenched when I looked at that empty black sky. It was eerie, and the sheep's behavior made it more so. Sheep are nervous creatures on a good night, startled from sleep if a neighbor shifts position. But this night they still slumbered. I have always scoffed at tales of sorcery, but now I wondered. Surely it was sorcery that had hidden our stars without scaring our sheep.

We clustered together, backs to the fire, staffs slippery in our freezing hands. But there was nothing to fight; no wolves or lions were attacking our sleeping flock. The only threat was the strange sky, and that was not a threat we could fight. The darkness grew, hovering over us, coming lower, blocking everything from our view. I found myself on my knees, frozen hands meeting frozen ground, hoping I would not embarrass myself by crying in front of my friends.

We're tough men, we shepherds, hardy and strong, immune to physical danger. We face wolves and lions with a staff and a sling, and climb down cliff sides to rescue fallen lambs. But this empty sky mocked my courage and made weakness of my strength. Glancing around, I saw my companions were also on their knees. We looked at each other, at the ground, at the sleeping sheep; anywhere to avoid looking again at that sky full of blackness that was creeping closer to us.

I rubbed my eyes, willing the tears I felt there not to fall; as cold as this night was, they would likely freeze on my face. Except I was no longer cold. At least, not the bitter cold I had felt during my rounds. The weather had shifted, and while I could still see my breath in the night air, I could also feel my fingers for the first time since starting my watch. It was easy now to grasp my staff, as I used it to help me stand. My stomach clenched again, wanting to empty itself of the dinner I had not yet eaten. What manner of night was this, when stars, sheep, nor weather behaved normally? Someone shouted behind me, and I whirled around, staff at the ready. Above the hills, the stars were back, jewels glittering in the clear sky.

For the third time I felt the grip of fear, and only my staff kept me from falling again. These were not *our* stars. A shepherd has many night watches, and he learns the stars and their seasons. Yahweh has ordered their paths in the sky and they do not shift from their assigned places as they move from one horizon to the other.

The stars we saw now were not in their usual places. I have never been so tempted to flee; never so willing to abandon the sheep I had sworn to protect. These stars were *moving*, almost dancing, careening into each other to form one larger, brighter star. *Yahweh protect me*, I breathed. It was not a larger, brighter star...whatever it was, it came ever closer to us, the brightness obscuring everything nearby, even my companions. Only the sound of their breathing told me they were still there.

The whatever-it-was stopped growing, but continued shining so brightly I had to shield my eyes. I heard music, more beautiful than any I've heard in my life. It made me forget the bitter cold winter, forget the Roman oppression and shattered dreams. Instead, I remembered springtime gardens and the warmth of the sun. The music ended, and I could finally see what had disturbed our night.

I tell you truly, I preferred the music and the springtime gardens to what I saw now. The creature before us was larger than any nephilim. Its radiance outshone the stars and our fire, making the black sky shine as bright as a mid-summer noon, and bathing our group in its light. "*David slew Goliath with a sling,"* I reminded myself, as my hand inched towards the pouch that held mine. But my arm froze in place, unable to move any closer to the pouch, no matter how I strained. The being spoke, and I heard echoes of the music in its voice.

"Do not be afraid," it said, and I almost laughed. How could we be anything *but* afraid on a night like this, when nothing was as it should be? And yet suddenly, as if simply from hearing those words, I was calm. No longer afraid, merely curious, wondering what would happen next.

"Fear not," it repeated. *"I have come with good news -- a baby has been born nearby. He will deliver you, for he is the Christ."*

The night air was cold in my open mouth, and it was only when I blinked my dry eyes that I realized I was staring. The angel -- surely this was an angel we were seeing, smiled at us.

"It's true!" He sang out. *"Your savior, the Christ, is born this very night. Go, see for yourselves. You'll find him swaddled and resting in a feed bin."*

The black sky was no longer oppressive, no longer crowding us to the ground. Instead, there were so many stars that the sky itself was hidden by them. No, these were not stars. These must be more angels joining the first, dancing and singing in celebration of this birth they announced. My heart knew their tune, and with tear-stained face I sang along: "Glory to God in the highest!"

Angelic descant added *"Peace on Earth!"* If anyone had said that to me at the start of my watch, I'd have laughed in his face. But now I felt that anything was possible. If our Messiah was here, as the angel declared he was, could peace be far behind?

I looked again at the sky and saw my familiar stars twinkling as the angels faded to a memory of light and music. Had I dreamt it? My heart answered "*no*" and I smiled as I remembered the Angelic descant. Peace on Earth, and the birth of our deliverer. It was a good time to be alive, a good time to be a shepherd in the hills near David's city. My friends' shouting interrupted my thoughts, and I hurried to join them as they ran to Bethlehem to find our Savior.

A Dream

It was a good day for dreaming. Warm sun on your back, a crisp tang in the air, clear water so cold that when you drink it your teeth hurt, sweet luscious grass to fill your tummy, and a shepherd to protect you. When a day is as perfect as that, what can a lamb do but sit and dream?

Jacob dreamed, and saw angels going back and forth to Heaven on a ladder of light. Abraham dreamed, and a great nation was born. And David, the shepherd-king -- his brothers didn't think he was good for anything except tending sheep, but God made him a mighty warrior, and a great king. They still talk about him around these parts. So I'm not ashamed of my dreaming, even if my friends **do** laugh.

Mind you, I'm not a lazy dreamer. I don't just lie there chewing my cud and think about where the greenest grass is. I dream about **real** things.

For instance, I dream that maybe someday I won't have to be afraid of the lions that wander the countryside, stealing my careless playmates. Lions look so cuddly from a distance -- I'd love to play with one. And if a lion were my friend, no other animal could hurt me, because the lion would protect me. I know it sounds silly. It's just a picture that pops into my head occasionally; me sleeping soundly, cuddled in the soft but deadly paws of my lion-friend, my head peeking out from his great ruff of fur. That would be such a warm, secure place, wouldn't it? So far it's just a dream, but it's a good dream, and worth wishing for, don't you think?

My other dream is kind of the same, only different. I dream that maybe someday the slaughter will stop, and we survivors won't have to listen to the cries of our innocent friends being killed because of someone else's crimes. Honestly, what could a sheep ever do to offend the almighty Jehovah? We're born, we run around in the fields, and eventually we die. We even give our wool to clothe the people around us, and we lighten their hearts when they watch our lambs play and jump in the joy of being alive. But they still kill us regularly, to protect themselves.

I know, it's not their fault, and it's not our Creator's fault. It's that sin-thing, that brought death into the world. Even so, sometimes when I'm lying here on a peaceful day, with no sounds of slaughter nearby, I dream about when innocent lambs will no longer be killed.

And this is a good dream, too. I know it in my heart, no matter what my friends say. And it will happen -- in fact, it **is** happening, which brings me back to that special day.

Actually, it wasn't the day as much as the evening that was special. We were all bedded down, under a coal-black sky, feeling secure behind our stone walls. Our shepherds were up by their fire, mostly, keeping warm. Of course, the scheduled watcher was making his rounds, soothing us to sleep with his quiet voice, naming each of us as he counted to make sure we were all safely in our fold.

I wasn't sleepy, so I had pushed my way to the outside edge, hoping for a friendly pat from the watcher. I could tell from his voice it was Ben, the shepherd who had charge of our group. Ben's my friend, and a fellow-dreamer. I especially like him because he talks to me as if I could understand him, instead of calling me a "dumb sheep."

I poked Ben with my nose, baaing softly. He scratched under my chin, where it always itches, but he wasn't paying attention to me. Instead, he was looking towards town.

There was a light over the town, like a small candle flickering or the glow from a faraway campfire. Only it couldn't have been a campfire, because it was in the sky, above a hillside.

As we both stared, the light grew brighter. Gradually, my eyes grew accustomed to the brilliance, and I could see it wasn't just a light, but was more like a star. The star's tail flickered, pulsing in and out, but it seemed to be pointing somewhere.

One of the other shepherds shouted, and Ben turned. I turned, too, keeping as close to Ben as I could get without knocking him over.

Away from the lights of the town, the sky should have been coal-black, with the clouds hiding our stars. Now it was as though a giant hand had brushed the clouds away, revealing all the stars that were ever created. But these stars weren't acting like stars. They were growing in size and brilliance, multiplying until they filled every corner of darkness, and there was nothing left but light. And in the radiance, I saw that they were not stars at all -- they were angels.

Like Father Jacob, I was given a vision of angels, but these weren't climbing to and from Heaven, they looked like they were playing, the way we lambs play in the spring. And as they leapt and did cartwheels and handsprings, their voices were lifted in a mighty chorus, singing praise to our Creator, and proclaiming his blessing on humanity. Caught up in their joy, I tried to do a back-flip, but there wasn't enough room, and I landed in front of Ben, who fell over me, but he quickly sat up and held me as we watched the angels slowly disappear, until we were left with only the glimmer of starlight and the memory of music too beautiful to describe.

Peering around Ben's shoulder, I saw the other star still hovered over the town. Its tail had grown until it reached the ground, a solid path of starlight, and I wondered if this was the ladder Jacob had seen, and if angels were even now climbing to and from Heaven by its glow.

Ben's friends were calling to him, and suddenly all the shepherds left the fold and ran towards the town. Ben ran, too, with me still in his arms, holding my breath lest he remember I was there and set me down.

I wanted to see this star path, and discover what sort of ladder it was, and who would be traveling on it between the heavens and the earth.

In town, we found a house bathed in starlight. The shepherds pounded on the closed door, calling for those inside to let them in. The man who opened it seemed surprised to see the shepherds, but they pushed forward, each of them trying to tell his story.

I kicked at Ben, and he set me down. Threading my way through his legs, I worked my way to the front of the group, and saw a woman lying down with a baby in her arms. I bleated a welcome to the new life, and she smiled at me. The shepherds stopped talking for a moment, and watched the man take the baby from her and place it in the feed bin, covering it with his robe.

The humans started talking again, but I wanted to see the baby. I raised up on my hind legs, resting my front feet on the edge of the manger, and poked my head over for a better look, but my eyes played tricks on me. Instead of a human baby, I saw a newborn lamb lying there, and it seemed I heard a whisper in my heart. *"Behold your dream, Josiah, the final innocent sacrifice."*

Like I said, my eyes were playing tricks, because even as I dropped back to all fours, that lamb became a human babe again.

The humans were still talking, but I wasn't listening. Suddenly too tired to move, I lay down beside the manger and closed my eyes.

With the gurgling and cooing of the child as a backdrop to the humans' talking, I fell asleep dreaming of a lamb who became a lion and slept beside me.

A Prophecy

I prostrated myself again, wondering at my audacity, but continuing my prayer.

"You are a God who keeps His promises," I reminded the Most High, "and you promised to send a Deliverer. Where is he, Yahweh? We've waited over 400 years -- will you make us wait a thousand?

"Keep your promise to your people: shine your glory on our land once again, and send us your deliverer."

I started to rise, but my muscles would not obey. The room glowed with the late afternoon sun, golden-pink heralding the sunset. I saw specks of dust dancing in a sunbeam, and they reminded me of the ladder Father Jacob saw. The glow faded and I could move again, but remained prostrate.

"Yahweh? Did you just speak to my heart? Did I really hear what you just promised me?"

As ever when my own words failed me, I relied on King David's: *"The king rejoices in your strength, O Lord, your victories bring him great joy!"* I wanted to dance in the streets of the city, the way David did when the Ark of the Covenant returned to Jerusalem.

"Should I tell anyone?" I wondered. *"Or is this message just for me?"*

Tell, I decided, so that all will believe when it comes true. I shared my story with the priest on duty, who called a scribe to record it. Walking home, I felt like my feet had wings, and if I only tried, I could walk among the stars. I could not stop smiling, and most people who passed me smiled back, enjoying my obvious joy.

Our Deliverer would arrive in *my* lifetime, and I would get to meet him! What a wondrous promise this was, and at the same time, how frustrating! Naturally, I expected the promise would be fulfilled in a very short time-frame. Yes, Yahweh is never in a hurry, but he knows that I am an impatient man, and I could not believe he would make me wait a lifetime. I was wrong about that.

Each time a new teacher drew crowds, I rushed to hear him, confident this time he would be our Deliverer. Each time, I was disappointed. Months turned to years, and years to decades, and I was still waiting.

"How long, O Lord? Will I be on my deathbed before your word is accomplished?"

I asked this question after every dashed hope, and Yahweh's answer never changed.

"Patience, my son. I have not forgotten you, not my promise to you."

It's easy to counsel patience when you can see all of time in one glance, but patience is difficult when you know you have a limited span of years on this earth, and you are watching the remainder become even shorter.

Sometimes I felt like Noah waiting for the rain to fall. He knew that Yahweh had spoken to him, but since the others hadn't heard, it was easy for them to doubt, and to share their doubts with him. Noah was faithful, and I would be faithful too, I promised myself. Yahweh had honored me with this promise, and I would be worthy of it.

Most of my life was behind me now, and while I was not yet on my deathbed, it seemed closer with every new day. Each day, it was a challenge to get out of bed. My joints creaked their protests, shooting pain at me that only eased when I sat still, soaking up the sun.

I no longer chased after every new teacher or rabbi, hoping to see my Messiah. Sooner or later, every teacher came to the Temple, so that was where I spent my days, waiting and watching; trying not to doubt the promise from my youth.

Did I really hear Yahweh? After all, there was no angelic messenger, no flash of fire or roar of thunder; just a thought in my mind, with all the assurance of tomorrow's sunrise. I recognized it as Yahweh, and called it His promise to me. But *was* it my Lord, or my imagination?

Yahweh has no idle words, no unfulfilled promises. But forty years later, I was still watching and waiting, wondering if this was the day I would see our Deliverer. Sometimes my heart failed me: with my ringing ears and dimming sight, would I hear him when he came? Would I be able to recognize him? Each time, Yahweh heard the fears in my heart, and each time, he reassured me.

"Do you think I would let him pass you by, Simeon my son? How then would you know your prayer had truly been answered? No my child, you will know him when you see him. I will not let your Messiah be unrecognized."

There were no new teachers in the Temple courtyard today, just an assortment of petitioners exchanging coinage or buying sacrificial animals. From what little I could see, most were for ritual purifications, but there were some consecrations. The sun was warm on my aching joints, and I soon slipped into sleep. I woke suddenly, thinking I had heard someone call my name. My heart was pounding as if I had been running. Through the ringing in my ears, I heard a baby cry.

My eyes watered from the bright sunlight, and I blinked quickly several times, wanting to see clearly. But what was I supposed to see?

"Yahweh?" I whispered in my mind. "Did you wake me?"

"It's today, Simeon. He's here now."

"Here? There are no new teachers here today."

Can our Creator laugh? I'm certain I heard him chuckle as he replied. *"Simeon, my son, I am doing a new thing, in a new way. Open your eyes, and see your Savior."*

My eyes *were* open, but all I could see was a young couple taking a baby to be consecrated. "I don't see him, Lord. Show me, please." I'm not sure what I expected with that prayer; maybe a flash of light to illuminate our Deliverer. Instead, I found myself remembering one of Isaiah's prophecies about a virgin and a baby. A baby?

I looked again at the young couple with their child. They looked like any other such, assaulted by the noise of the daily Temple business. The man appeared to be searching for something: his wife stood beside him, holding the babe close to her breast.

Normally, the process of standing was slow and painful for me, as I eased each creaking joint to a new position. This time, I didn't even notice as I stood and walked over to them.

"Welcome to Jerusalem," I said. They started, not expecting anyone to speak to them. "The Temple area can be confusing. Can I help you find something?"

"We're here to consecrate our son," the father replied. "I'm looking for the dove-seller."

"Congratulations to you both. A son is a blessing from Yahweh."

They shared a glance and smile before nodding. My heart felt like it was going to push through my skin, it was pounding so.

"May I see him?" It was a bold question for a stranger to ask, but it did not seem to surprise them.

The babe had been asleep, but as she shifted his position to give me a better view, his eyes opened. Some babies are fretful when they wake, but he wasn't. He made a little baby coo of surprise, and then he saw me and smiled.

I am an old man, and I have seen many babies through the years. But when this one smiled at me, I felt like I was once again a little babe myself, with my parents applauding my first steps and my first words. There was still no beacon of light, no thunderclap proclamation of glory, but I was not surprised to feel tears on my face. I knew it was not the sun making my eyes water this time: I was overwhelmed by a sense of being loved.

The babe's mother was watching me closely, probably wondering about this old man who cried when he looked at a baby.

"Is anything wrong?" she asked me.

I could not speak for joy. I'm certain I looked like a madman, clapping my hands, almost dancing in place, tears falling into my beard even as I laughed. I finally recovered enough to reassure them.

"Yahweh is so good to us! This day, I have seen his promise fulfilled in the smile of an infant. May I hold him?"

They looked at each other, then she handed him to me. Holding him, I was filled again with the sense of being loved. I hadn't planned to say anything, but Yahweh filled my mouth with words of praise and blessing.

As I handed the child back to her, I found I did not want to let him go. I wanted to keep him with me for eternity. And then Yahweh gave me one more message, this time for the young mother.   I embraced her as a father would his daughter, and spoke words of awe and dread.

"Your child is appointed and destined for greatness, but a sword will pierce your heart." I choked on my tears, and could not say more.

I wanted to tell her not to worry, that her son was the Messiah, and that Yahweh never forgets a promise. That no sword would ever take away the joy that He had given her, and that love cannot be conquered by the hatred of men, but the look in her eyes told me she already knew that.

I turned to leave, whispering again the words I had first spoken when I held my Deliverer. "Lord, now let your servant go in peace, for your promise has been fulfilled. I, an ordinary everyday man, have seen my savior. I have held you in my arms, O Lord. Hold me now in yours, for eternity."

A Visit

We explain the incomprehensible, and uncover the mysteries within the mundane. This has been our task for centuries, and we are experts at what we do. So when I tell you that we encountered something never before recorded by any of us, you understand how unusual that was.

The stars hold our future and our past. They detail the seasons, warn us of weather patterns, and guide us in our travels. We spend our nights engrossed in the sky's display, and explain its portents to our rulers. But this display was not easy to comprehend. We woke our oldest member to see if he could explain it. He is older than most grandfathers, and his eyesight is failing, but when we pointed him towards the western sky, he gasped as we had done.

"What does it mean?" His creaky voice was barely a whisper, but we knew his question. It was the same question we had been asking ourselves since it first appeared.

"We don't know," we told him. "Do you?" His hand on my arm trembled, and I guided him to a bench before his legs failed him.

"Such a thing has never been seen." We had crowded near to hear his whisper, and groaned almost in unison.

"Remember our precepts," he admonished us. "We study; we learn; we know." His voice grew stronger as the familiar litany pulled him into the teaching role he had long forsaken.

"Have we studied?" His tone was as sharp as during my apprenticeship.

"Yes, Master" we chorused, just as during our apprentice days.

"What have we learned?"

The silence lengthened as we pondered. Had we learned anything? His cane rapped the stone.

"Come, come! I taught you better than this. When did it appear? Was there any warning of it?"

Silence turned to cacophony, and he pounded his cane again.

"Shame! You have let a mystery un-nerve you. And you call yourselves learned men." He had apparently forgotten that he was also un-nerved at first. As he pointed to each of us, we shared our findings; and I for one did not resent being relegated to apprentice status. This mystery *did* un-nerve me, and I had no idea what it might be.

The familiar routine of sharing our findings calmed me, as it did my colleagues. It had appeared without warning one night, blazing in the western sky, its brilliance hiding the stars we normally saw there. Each night it seemed brighter, pulsing with an intensity that demanded our attention. We knew when it first appeared, we knew how long it shone each night, and when it intensified. We knew exactly when the morning sun would hide its brilliance. The only thing we didn't know was what it meant.

We found the answer in a centuries old prophecy. I should have known Daniel would have been the one to tell us. His name is still legend among us, both for his accuracy and his steadfast adherence to his own god. He also left us a record of his people's unfulfilled prophecies, and in that record we found our answer. This was a star announcing Israel's new king, who would rival the greatness of their greatest kings of old. Wishing to honor the new king, we packed our caravan with princely gifts and headed west.

The desert sun baked the sand and the chill nights were a welcome relief from the unending heat. I longed for the coolness of my garden, the fragrance of jasmine on the evening air. But my longing faded every time I looked at that pulsing star, its brilliance heightened by the darkness of the desert nights.

Herod's palace was ordinary, compared to some I've seen, but that was perhaps to be expected. Jews cared more about their god than any human king, after all. But what really surprised me was how calm everyone was.

Surely such a birth as the stars announced would have occasioned celebrations, but there were no special activities here. We were weeks on the way, but still, the celebrations should have been ongoing. What little gossip we heard as we waited for our audience with Herod was about local affairs, not a new baby.

We bowed deeply before the king.

"What brings such esteemed visitors to our humble land?" He asked.

Our leader answered for us. "We have come with all haste to give honor and glory to the new-born king of Israel, long may he reign."

After a moment of stunned silence, Herod clapped his hands and guards surrounded us, penning us in place while the hall emptied. When we were alone, he clapped again, and the guards retreated to the back of the hall, giving us privacy.

"A new-born king, you say?" Herod's voice was calm, but he was not smiling. "I'm afraid you're mistaken. There are no babies here."

"But there must be!"

"The star!"

"The prophecies!"

Several of my fellows spoke at once, quieting when Herod raised his hands. Our leader glared at them, then bowed again.

"If the king has the time to hear our tale, I would start at the beginning..." He paused for his response.

"Tell me everything you know," he said.

So he did, starting with the unexpected star and ending with our research into the prophecies Daniel had left with us. Herod absorbed our explanations with no expression on his face, cold eyes staring at each of us in turn. His eyes reminded me of a cobra, and I was glad I was an emissary of Persia, rather than one of his subjects. He bade us wait while he conferred with his own scholars.

We waited quietly. I can't speak for my colleagues, but I spent the hours reviewing all we had learned since we first saw the new star, and remembering all I had ever heard about King Herod.

He was smiling when he came back to us, but his cobra-eyes were still cold and hard.

"You misunderstood the prophecy," he told us. "The prince you seek to honor was not born in Jerusalem, but in a nearby village. Go to Beit-lechem, find this young princeling, and bring me the details so that I can also worship him. I would go myself, but it is better that I stay here and prepare the celebration."

Our leader agreed, and we left the splendor of Jerusalem for the poverty of a peasant village. It was near dark when we arrived, so we camped outside the village, with hundreds of others.

The Prince's star haunted my dreams, alternately exalting and depressing me. I kept seeing Herod's cold eyes, imagining that cobra stare directed towards the infant prince, and I feared for him. But when we found the prince, my fears melted into wonder. He was just a baby, maybe a year old, maybe a little older. I study stars, not babies. I don't know that I've been this close to one before, close enough to be enthralled by his lively eyes and toothless grin. I held him, and he reached for the chain around my neck, pulling my medallion into his mouth. His mother pulled him away, apologizing. Laughing, I retrieved him from her, and he again placed my medallion in his mouth, gumming it with all his might.

I did not want to hand him back to his mother, or to my colleagues. I wanted to keep him with me forever, to protect him from the poison in Herod's cobra-eyes, to help him grow into his kingship. I bounced him on my knee, laughing again at his joy. Knowing we had to leave, I drew him to me for one last embrace. Our eyes met, and time disappeared.

I looked into this princeling's eyes, and saw our world as if I were viewing it from among the stars. The sky was storm-cloud black, and the earth was weeping, her tears falling as rain on a muddy hillside. There was a cave nearby, and Roman soldiers were blocking its entrance with a giant boulder. Sorrow drove the strength from my limbs and I staggered. That quickly, the child threw his arms wide and leapt from me towards his mother's arms, crowing his delight as she caught him mid-flight. The vision faded, replaced with an assurance that all was well, that all would be well. As I rested my hand on his fuzzy head in farewell, I knew two things. The stars were right in their declaration that the world was changing, and there was no way I would help Herod find this child.

I said as much to my colleagues on our way back to our campsite, and was shocked when they disagreed.

"We are emissaries for our people," our leader said. "We must keep our promise to Herod."

"He doesn't want to honor this new prince," I protested.

"You don't know that," he replied. "There is no evidence for your conclusion."

"No evidence?" I stared at him. "His history is all the evidence we need! Herod does not tolerate rivals. If he finds this baby, he will kill him."

"Men change. And we promised. We must keep our word."

"Do none of you see how wrong he is?" I appealed to the group, my heart aching. "We must protect this babe, so he can grow up and become the king the stars foretold."

"We do not meddle," our leader said. The others murmured agreement. "We observe; we study, and we learn. We advise, but we never interfere. You know this."

"We advise." I agreed. "And I'm advising you - *do not tell Herod*. We should just go home."

"We *are* going home. By way of Jerusalem, where we will honor our promise, and let King Herod know we have found his heir."

"NO." I had no more words than this. "I will not."

"You would return alone? The desert is dangerous for lone travelers."

"And Herod is dangerous for this babe. I will not go with you to Jerusalem. I cannot." I walked away from them, taking my bedroll to the edge of our camp and spreading it there, to emphasize my decision. I heard the normal sounds of the camp preparing for the night, but saw none of it. I kept my back to them, staring into the desert. The stars winked at me as the sky faded to black. I did not see the one that proclaimed the new king; it was on the other side of the camp. But I saw it in my mind, re-living the wonder and fear of its first appearance, when we didn't know its message.

Our leader spoke truly. We examine and explain, sometimes advising, but we do not interfere. What happens, happens. Was it interfering if we did not tell Herod, or was telling him the interference? I wasn't sure. I wished I had someone to advise me, but all I had was the certainty in my

heart, and the assurance that all would be well. Clinging to that assurance, and remembering the happy giggles of the child, I closed my eyes.

The star shone in my dream, blazing even brighter than when we had first seen it. The light dazzled, and I had to shield my eyes. I saw the babe, held him on my knee again, smiling at his joy in life. He started crying, and disappeared. I searched frantically, but to no avail. There was nothing to see but the desert sand, the black sky, and the star with its long tail reaching the ground. The star gleamed like burnished copper, its tail blood-red. As I watched, unable to move, the tail changed to a cobra, slithering through the streets of a small village. I tried to warn them, but the same power that froze my limbs stole my voice. I could only watch helplessly as the cobra entered each house, seeking its prey.

The stars dimmed, as if a veil had been drawn across them, leaving only the king-star, now pulsing blood-red. In the distance a baby cried, the sound muffled by the wails of many mothers, and the shouts of my companions. Their shouts woke me. I shook my head, trying to push the remnants of the dream away.

The stars shone normally in the sky above me, not veiled as in my dream. The black sky was beginning to lighten with the approach of the new day. The king-star was still there, bright silver-white as it had been since we first saw it. My colleagues rushed to me, insisting I tell them my dream. I had barely started before they interrupted, claiming their dreams had been identical.

I looked at our leader, and he nodded. When we broke camp, we turned our backs on the brightness that had guided us for so long, heading home via a route that went nowhere near Jerusalem.

Epilogue

"Joseph? With the gifts those kings gave us, we could go home now." We had talked about returning to Nazareth, but wanted a donkey for the trip. The kings had been generous, and we could buy a donkey now.

I smiled at the thought of introducing Yshua to my parents. Mama would cry with joy, and then she would wipe her eyes and prepare a feast. All our friends and relatives would drop by, rejoicing in our safe return.

"Please, Joseph." I laid my hand on his arm. "Say we can leave soon." He patted my hand.

"We'll need to buy a donkey," he said.

Two days later, he brought home a donkey. I stroked her neck, and whispered into her long ears, telling her how happy I was to see her. She shook her head and stomped a back foot on the ground, and Joseph pulled me away.

"She's not a pet, Mary. She's a donkey. Please be careful."

"When will you leave?" Deborah and Ezra had been admiring the donkey as well, and the question was Deborah's.

"Tomorrow is Shabbat," Joseph replied. "So we'll wait until the next day."

I was happy to think of leaving so soon, but sad, too. The months we had spent with them made Ezra and Deborah as precious to me as my own family.

At dinner, I only ate a few bites. The lump in my throat made it hard to swallow.

"Is anything wrong?" Deborah asked me. You've barely touched your meal."

I blushed. "I was just thinking of how precious all of you are to me now, and how much I will miss you."

She smiled. "We'll miss you, too. But you should eat -- you'll need your strength for traveling, and for your precious son."

I knew she was right, but my aching heart stole my appetite.

"I didn't expect leaving to be so hard," I told Joseph that night. "I'm anxious to see Mama, but the thought of leaving here...these months have been so wonderful."

He hugged me, and I leaned into him, enjoying the feel of his arms around me.

"It'll be all right, love. It's always hard to say goodbye when you care for someone. But we still have tomorrow; we're not leaving yet."

I didn't understand how I could be excited and sad at the same time, and while I was trying to make sense out of it, I fell asleep. Joseph's voice startled me awake, ending a dream where Mama was helping Yshua take his first steps toward me.

"Mary!" He called again. "Wake up! We must leave now."

"What?" I rubbed my eyes, but the room was still dark. There was no hint of dawning, just the solid black of deep night.

"We must leave now," he repeated.

"Joseph, it's the middle of the night! We can't sneak out like thieves."

"We must." He insisted. "We're not safe here."

He was already up, gathering our belongings while we talked.

"Joseph!" I tried to keep my voice low, but it was too late. Ezra and Deborah brought a lamp into the room with them, and I saw the strain in Joseph's face. He turned to them.

"I'm sorry we woke you."

"What is it?" Ezra asked. "Why are you packing?"

"We must leave now. It's not safe here." Before they could ask Joseph the same questions I did, he continued.

"Yahweh sent an angel in to my dreams tonight to warn me. We must leave this very night if we want our child to live."

"An angel in your dreams," Deborah repeated. "Like the last time?"

He nodded. "Exactly. I can't ignore the warning. We must go."

They nodded. We had told them about the dream Yahweh sent, telling Joseph that I didn't lie about the baby.

"You'll need food." Deborah said. "It's a long way to Nazareth."

"We're not going to Nazareth." We all stared at him.

"Then where?" I asked, not wanting to hear the answer. I wanted to go home, to see Mama and let her meet her grandson. I wanted to tell them all that happened on that wonderful night Yshua was born, and about the grandfather at the Temple.

Joseph took a deep breath before answering. "Egypt. We'll be safer there."

"Safer? In the land of Pharaoh? Joseph, are you sure?"

He looked at me, and smiled. "I know it sounds crazy, but the Angel said Egypt."

"Good thing you bought that donkey," Ezra said as he started to leave. "I'll go get her ready for you."

"Thank you." Joseph turned to me. "Mary, I know you wanted to go home, but --" I interrupted him.

"We must heed Yahweh's warnings, Joseph. I'd rather go home, but I understand."

It seemed like no time until the donkey was packed and we stood beside her, ready to leave.

"I will miss you," Deborah said as she hugged me.

"And I, you. Thank you, Deborah, for everything."

"It was our joy. Yahweh go with you, and guide you."

"And with you, and keep you safe."

Deborah held Yshua while Joseph helped me mount, then handed him to me. As soon as we were securely settled, Joseph led the donkey away.

We walked quietly through the dark village. Yshua slept in my arms, and the stars brightened the sky above us, a sliver of moon helping us see. We paused on the edge of town, looking at each other.

"This is it, then," I thought. "Goodbye to all we love, and hello to an unexpected future."

"Are you all right?" He asked me. "I know this wasn't what you had hoped for."

I sighed. "Will we ever go home again, Joseph?"

"In time, love. Yahweh will send us, when the time is right."

I sighed again, then smiled at him, pushing my disappointment away.

"Well then I'm even more grateful for those gifts the kings gave us. They should tide us over until the Egyptians discover your skills."

He smiled at me, and kissed Yshua's forehead. Then he tugged on the donkey's lead-rope and we headed into the unknown.

Scripture References

for

the Stories You Just Read

You might already know the Biblical versions of the Christmas story, but if you don't, you can find them in the first two chapters of both Matthew & Luke.

I used their writings to fuel my imagination. Obviously, not every story in this collection can point to a Scripture verse, but I hope you enjoyed them just the same.

Thank You

Thank you for purchasing **Through Hope's Eyes**. I hope and pray that reading these stories has blessed you as much as writing them has blessed me.

This particular group of stories began when I was attending Abundant Life Church in San Antonio, Texas. For several years, Pastor Gerald Ripley allowed me to share my stories with the congregation during the Christmas season. I don't know that I ever intended them to be a book, but I'm glad they are, and I hope you're glad too.

As I worked on these stories, I was surprised to realize I was almost afraid to share them in a book. I can hear you thinking: *What could be scary about Christmas stories?*

Simply this: everyone knows them, and expects any new treatments to match what they already know. Like many Americans, I grew up watching Christmas specials on TV every year. Long-eared donkeys and miniature musicians featured prominently in those specials, but there was always a barn and a feed-bin, because the inn was full.

Church Christmas pageants reinforced the same images, and there have been countless sermons preached about making room in your heart for the baby who had no room when he was born.

When I was writing the stories for this book, I had fun imagining the back-stories of the key players while striving to remain true to the events described by Matthew & Luke.

I especially enjoyed writing the segment I wrote with the innkeeper and his wife, right before the birth. You didn't get to read that segment, because even though it was a joy to write, it didn't make it to the final version of the book.

Just because something is traditional doesn't mean it's true, and as much as I love the image of a feed-bin in a barn, I'm no longer convinced it's accurate.

I've learned that a manger doesn't automatically mean there was a stable. In that time, families had a manger in the common room of their home, because they brought their animals inside at night. The word that we have been told means *"inn"* is more often translated as *"guest chamber."* It's actually the same word that is translated elsewhere as *"upper room"* when Jesus and the disciples were looking for a place to have their Passover Seder.

I've said it before: I'm not a Bible scholar, and I don't pretend to be one. But from the time I learned about the more accurate translation of *"katalyma,"* I wasn't satisfied with my innkeeper segment, and had to re-write it to reflect my new understanding.

It's scary to go against traditional Christmas concepts, but I like the difference it made in the stories for this book. I hope you do, too.

A Bonus Christmas Story

This bonus story, "*The Vigil*" is one of the stories I shared with my church family in Texas. It was written as a performance piece for two players. I call it a "double soliloquy" for lack of a better description.

The Vigil

A double soliloquy

The Place: Two rooftops at opposite ends of a small town.

The Time: Night. Specifically, the silent hours between midnight and dawn, when fears are magnified, doubts intensified, and courage hardest to find. The kind of night when you wrestle with angels, or with yourself.

The Players: An engaged couple.

Author's Note:

When we consider Advent, we're pondering the coming of Jesus, mostly by reflecting on His birth, and the events leading up to it.

Over the centuries, the nativity has been sanitized. We emphasize the miracles: Elizabeth, the star, the virgin birth. And we're right to do so, for surely this is a season of miracles. But sometimes we forget the reality in the midst of the miraculous.

The reality: parents whose teenage daughter is pregnant out of wedlock.

The reality: a man finds out that his fiancée is pregnant, and knows he's not the father.

These are some of the realities that God used to create the miracle we call Christmas. They're not really all that different from the realities of our daily lives. Which gives us another reason for hope, in this season when hope reigns triumphant. Knowing how God has used past realities as the setting for awesome miracles renews our hope that He can work the same miracles in our own lives, with our present realities

.

(Narrator)

This is how the birth of Jesus the Messiah came about: His mother Mary was pledged to be married to Joseph, but before they came together, she was found to be pregnant through the Holy Spirit.

Because Joseph her husband was faithful to the law, and yet did not want to expose her to public disgrace, he had in mind to divorce her quietly. Matthew 1:18-19

****

(Joseph enters, agitated)

"I will lift up mine eyes unto the hills, from whence cometh my help..."

Are you there, God? My help is supposed to come from you, who made Heaven and Earth.

Why didn't you help me?

You know how I love her, how I've believed that you were the one who chose her for me, as you chose Rebekah for Isaac. Didn't you hear **any** of my prayers for her?

"Watch over my beloved," I asked you. *"Guard and protect this woman you have given me."*

Where was your protection when it happened? If you are indeed with us always, then why didn't you stop it? Stop **her**?

My thoughts are chasing each other like sawdust in the breeze, and none of them make sense.

I'm so angry I can't see straight, but my anger has no outlet.

I can't be angry at you, because I know that your ways are not our ways, and that I cannot begin to search out the secrets of your mind.

To be angry with her is like being angry with myself, she's so much a part of me. And yet, I **am** angry with her.

If she didn't want to marry me, she had only to speak, and I would have released her. Love doesn't force people, and I would never force Mary.

But why would she say she loved me, if she didn't? And what caused the joy that lit up her eyes so they sparkled every time she saw me, if not love?

Why would she say "yes" to me, if not for love? I have no wealth to give her, other than the depth of my love and whatever my work may provide.

No, she **had** to love me when she agreed to be my wife.

Didn't she?

(Joseph freezes)

*(**Mary** enters, dreamily)*

If I knew how to put words on parchment, I would write down for you all the emotions I carry in my heart.

The joy that springs up when you look at me in that special way.

The amazement that you would choose me to share your life.

The love I have for you, so strong that sometimes I think it will overcome me, and nothing of myself would remain, except this great, all-powerful love.

If I were a scribe or poet, I would write these things for you, to declare my love for all time.

But I am only a girl, untrained in the use of quill and scroll.

If I were brazen and forward, I would stand by the well in the morning, when the women come with their jugs for water, and I would shout my love for all the world to hear.

But we would both be embarrassed by such a display, and our love would stop being a noble, beautiful gift, and become instead a cheap, tawdry thing, whispered about and laughed at in every corner where people gather.

Even my parents, who love me more than life itself, do not fully understand this bond we have, that transcends a mere betrothal and reaches to the very gates of Heaven.

So with no one to talk to about how wonderful you are, and how much I love you, I look up to the stars, and their twinkles seem like understanding smiles, urging me to speak to them of my beloved.

(Mary freezes)

(Joseph)

I watched you grow up, and you never knew I was watching. You were the smile on your mother's face, the proud gleam in your father's eyes.

You fell outside my shop one day, and I carried you inside, where my mother tended your bruises.

You were so light in my arms, almost no weight at all. You rested your head against my shoulder, and I knew that I wanted you to always remain there, leaning on me as your protector.

When I helped you home, and you told your parents I was a new friend, I felt a strange emotion stir in my heart. I grinned all the way back to my shop, and Mother said she had never seen me look so happy.

Your friendship brought joy into my life, and your smiles were rays of sunshine on cloudy days.

You grew older, and I began to ask God if you were the one for me, the person he had created to share my life.

(Joseph freezes)

(Mary)

When you first visited my father's house, to talk about doing some work for him... I talked to the stars that night, describing your strength and gentleness, marveling that two such different qualities could exist in one man.

And your eyes – there was a moment we both glanced at each other. The world stood still, and all noise stopped. Nothing existed for me except your brown eyes, and the tender love I surprised there.

My father had to speak your name twice before we were able to break our gaze, and my mother wondered the rest of the day about the smile I could not quite hide.

These stars of mine know all about you, my beloved, and about us. When the secrets of my heart seem so great as to burst from holding everything in, I retreat to a place where I can see them smile at me, and tell them about us.

I told them about our betrothal, when it was formalized. Honestly, I would have told anyone who would listen, except everyone already knew.

Giddy with joy, almost drunk with the force of my love for you, I laughed and giggled until my mother feared I'd lost my wits.

And you, my tall carpenter, stood there beside me, strong and serene, smiling. I love your smile, the way it starts slowly and grows until it seems to light the room. My friends were afraid you'd be too serious for me, but then, they'd never seen your smile.

(Mary freezes)

(Joseph)

What happened then? Did your love grow cold since the betrothal, waiting for a wedding that seemed like it would never come?

Am I to blame for insisting we wait until our house is finished? But each time we spoke of it, you seemed content to wait.

Surely I would have noticed some frustration, or seen the love dying in your beautiful eyes. But I saw nothing.

I guess they're right when they say love is blind. I was certainly blinded by my love for you, imagining you cared as deeply as I did.

Even today, when you came to the shop, your face almost shouted your joy at our reunion. I can't believe that could happen without love.

But then we walked, and you shattered my world.

(Joseph freezes)

(Mary)

Oh my love, I begged Yahweh for a short betrothal. We were practically married already, and I had no doubts about the rightness of our union. From the day you entered my life, all I wanted was to keep house for you, to be your helper, to give you a family.

The stars know the dreams I've had, whispered to them under the cover of darkness when my parents thought I was asleep.

My last thoughts every night are of you, my love. I fall asleep with your name on my lips, and wake every morning whispering hello to you.

Your love is a most precious gift for me – in its depth, its breadth, its faithfulness. Your love for me is steadfast, surpassed only by the love of Yahweh.

At least, I hope it is. Joseph, I do not know how to make you believe me. Even my stars are hiding their faces from me tonight, but I've done nothing wrong.

I don't know what I was thinking when I said yes. Not to you, but to Yahweh that day. If I had known then that it would cost me your love, would I still have agreed?

Today, when I came home from my cousin's house, I was still excited by the miracle of her new son. Imagine, having a child when you're past the age of childbearing! Only Jehovah God could bring life to her dead womb. And her baby – Joseph, he knew even before I did about my baby. I was still in shock over the angel's words, trying to convince myself that it wasn't a dream. Why would Yahweh choose me, a girl who is barely a woman, to carry out his plan?

But the angel – Gabriel – he said that I had found favor with Yahweh, and I would be blessed among women. When he told me I would bear the Messiah, I was confused.

"I've never been with a man." I said (please believe that, my beloved). *"How could this happen to me?"*

Joseph, my love, he told me that the Holy Spirit and Jehovah God would fill me, and that my son would be called "the Son of God."

What could I say? Thanks for thinking of me, but I'd rather not?

Of course I agreed. Shyly, hesitantly, and with a thousand questions in my mind. If you could have seen this angel, you'd have done the same. When I gazed on him, all my questions disappeared, and I was bathed in the love of Jehovah God.

But once the angel left, the questions returned. And the biggest question was you. Would you believe my child was from God? I knew the townspeople would judge me, and gossip about me. But they don't matter.

You are what matters – your opinion is the one I live or die by. Will you believe me?

(Mary freezes)

(Joseph)

Mary!

My soul is on fire, but my heart is a frozen block of ice.

From the moment I heard those words "I am with child," I became a dead man.

My dreams of our life together, our family, are as dead as the wood I use for making tables, and will never live again.

Yahweh! Jehovah God!

How can I bear this pain, having that which I most long for torn away from me, knowing that everything she said was a lie?

She said she loved me, that she desired nothing more than to be my wife. Then how could she do this to me?

Where was her love **then**?

She denies being attacked, so she must have been willing, but if she truly loved me, how could she be willing? And if she wasn't willing, why is she lying about it? Who is she protecting? But how could she be willing, and still claim she loves me?

And then to blaspheme, as if lying weren't enough. Claiming that Yahweh chose **her** to be mother of the Messiah.

She must be losing her mind. Nothing good ever comes out of Nazareth.

(Joseph freezes)

(Mary)

The night is so dark with my friendly stars hiding. And so long, while I wait for your decision.

I came home from Elizabeth's today, and even before going to my parents' house, I ran to find you, to share my excitement with you.

I was so happy to see you, Beloved – it felt like we'd been apart years instead of weeks.

Your eyes lit up when you saw me, and you were almost rude to your customer, trying to get him to leave so you could greet me. Suddenly shy, I stayed by the door. You crossed the distance between us in two great strides, ready to grab me and whirl me around in your joy, when I killed your smile with a question.

"Joseph, could you walk with me? We need to talk."

As we left the crowded areas, I began to share with you what I had seen and heard. Each word seemed to slow our pace, as if our feet and my sentences had an agreement, and my story ended at the same time our walk did.

You only looked at me twice – once when I began my story, and again when I was finished.

Your eyes searched my soul, while I searched your eyes for love, and found only anger at my betrayal. It was clear that you didn't believe me, that you thought I was making up a story to hide my sin.

I waited as your love struggled with your hurt, and lost.

"I need some time to think about this," you said. *"I'll tell you tomorrow what steps I will take."*

Why is the night so **long**? Will morning **never** come?

Are you sleeping, my love, or are we keeping this vigil together, both searching our hearts, both waiting for the sun to roll back the darkness covering the land?

But what will chase the darkness from my heart if you put me away?

Jehovah God, you are the father of this child growing within me. You called me "blessed among women", and declared that I had found favor with you.

I know it was not a dream, a delusion created to cover a foolish mistake. You are El Shaddai, protector and defender of all Israel. I need your protection, Lord God, for I am defenseless against my Joseph's anger.

He doesn't believe me, Lord. I saw the love in his eyes turn to judgment. And if my beloved doesn't believe me, who will protect me from the looks and the gossip?

So I've failed you. Your child will be an outcast, the product of a deluded woman. I will be cast aside, and either pitied for my delusions or reviled for my loose behavior.

Was I deluded? Was there **really** an angel with robes of fire, and a face of pure love? **Did** I hear him correctly?

How can I doubt when the truth grows within me each day?

Joseph, my love, you must believe me. But you have hidden your love from me, as the stars have hidden their light, leaving me alone.

(Mary freezes)

(Joseph)

Oh, Mary, don't you know I **want** to believe you? Tell me something believable, and I will stand beside you.

But I cannot support your delusions. For if these are not lies you've made up, then you have surely become unbalanced.

Yahweh. Does. **NOT.** SPEAK to People! Not today. Not in 400 years.

And if he **did** choose to break his silence, don't you think he would have chosen someone else? Someone more qualified?

Like a **priest**, perhaps? Someone trained to recognize his voice, and to interpret it correctly?

Maybe even someone from Bethlehem, where the Messiah is supposed to be born?

You're asking more than I can give, my love, to expect I could enter into your delusions and treat them as truth.

To put you away would be like tearing the heart from my chest, but to marry you, and raise another man's child as my own?

I don't know if I can do it.

(Joseph freezes)

(Mary)

El Shaddai, you have promised from Eternity that you will never leave your people. Be with me now, Lord, and give me the strength to bear this blessing you have given me. Even in this darkest night, with my world crumbling around me, I cling to your promise and my commitment.

Behold the handmaiden of the Lord. Be it unto me according to your will. With or without my Joseph, I am your servant, and will trust in you.

Help me when it hurts, Lord God, and protect me from the scorn of those I love. From the look in my Joseph's eyes.

I have **never** known a night to pass so slowly.

Joseph, beloved, no matter what you decide, you will always live in my heart, and I will never stop loving you. I would give anything to spare you the pain of this night, but I cannot say no to Yahweh.

So make your decision, my friend, whichever way you will, and Yahweh will give me the strength to accept it.

(Mary freezes)

(Joseph)

I don't know if I can spend my life wondering who the real father is, and whether Mary loved him instead of me.

Or have an arranged marriage, without love. I know that many people do, but I wanted more.

Was I asking too much, God? After all, Jacob loved Rachel, and they were allowed to marry. If I put her away, what will happen to her? Who would take her in? Would they stone her? That **is** the legal punishment.

I can't put her away. What would happen to me? Knowing that the woman I loved needed me and I turned her away? What kind of man would do that?

But what kind of woman would break her vows? How can I ever trust her again? She won't tell me who the father is (except to claim it's Jehovah God), but children look like their parents.

So the child would grow, daily mocking me with the evidence of his true parentage. Can **any** man live like that? Surely God doesn't expect me to marry her.

But to not marry her.... to not see her when she first wakes in the morning, rubbing the sleep from her eyes. To never again see her smile chase the clouds away, or hear the music of her laughter. I would only be half a man.

I cannot love her any more, and yet I cannot stop loving her. My heart is hers, even though we'll never wed.

I'll tell her parents tomorrow, and move my shop to another town, to start over.

(Joseph freezes)

(Mary)

My beloved Joseph, all the love I have ever felt for you is as nothing compared to the love I have for you at this very moment. My other love for you seems so small and selfish next to this new and greater love. I wonder if this is like Yahweh's love for us, so full and overflowing that there's no room for doubts and fears.

Thank you, Yahweh, for the grandeur of your love, which does not depend on whether it's returned. Thank you for the babe you've given me, the trust and honor you've shown. And thank you for my Joseph, for the chance to know what it's like to be treasured and cherished. I don't know all of your plan for me and your Messiah, but I am your handmaiden to the end.

Precious stars, you're shining on me again. Shine on my Joseph, and kiss his face with your starlight. Caress him with your moonbeams. Gentle breeze, whisper my love for him in his ears as he sleeps. Tell him that I understand.

The night is almost gone, and I no longer fear the day. Yahweh will provide, no matter what Joseph decides. I could sleep now, peacefully resting in the love of El Shaddai, but I think I'll wait for the sunrise, and describe it to little Yshua – the Morning of Love, I'll call it, with the Dawn of Hope.

****

(Narrator)

"...an angel of the Lord appeared to him in a dream and said, "Joseph son of David, do not be afraid to take Mary home as your wife, because what is conceived in her is from the Holy Spirit. She will give birth to a son, and you are to give him the name Jesus, because he will save his people from their sins." Matthew 1:20-21

If you liked the stories in this book, you might want to read *Through Love's Eyes*, which picks up this story line approximately 30 years later. Turn the page for a preview of *Through Love's Eyes*.

Preview: Through Love's Eyes

A Woman Who was Spared

We all make bad choices, and mine almost got me killed. I was young then, and widowed. While that might explain my choice, it does not excuse it, even though I have always used that as my excuse. But Yahweh did not say "this is the law unless you are young and widowed," he said "this is the law." Knowing that, understanding that, how could I choose as I did? I've never been able to really answer that question. I just chose.

Life is hard for a widow, even if she has no children. He found me at a time when I needed help, and assisted me. I thanked him and Yahweh for his assistance, and offered him a cool drink in gratitude.

He closed the door behind him as he entered my tiny house, his large frame filling the small room as my husband had once done. He sat down at the table where I placed the cup, his eyes taking in every aspect of my home, and of me. My face grew warm as he looked at me, and my voice trembled when I reassured him that I had plenty of juice if he was still thirsty.

"If you have plenty, pour some for yourself and join me," he invited, gesturing at the other chair.

"I really should –" but he interrupted me with a smile.

"Should what? Cook? Clean? No, what you should do" and he stressed the "should" with his voice, "is to join me in this cup you've given me."

He grinned, an open inviting grin, and gestured to the chair again. "I'll tell no one that you took a mid-day break, if that's what worries you."

The jug clinked against the cup as I poured my juice. My hands were shaking so much I was afraid I would spill it. It had been a long time since a man's voice had been heard in my house, a long time since a man's eyes had appraised me. Rising, he took the jug from me, insisting that I sit down before I fell.

"I'm sorry."

"You are not well," he said. "It's good that I happened by when I did."

His hands were gentle as he helped me to the chair, wrapping my own hands around the cup.

"Drink." He commanded, and like an obedient child, I tried to lift the cup to my lips. He caught it before it spilled, and held it for me so I could drink. I closed my eyes against the nearness of his face, and breathed in his fragrance.

"Men smell differently than women," I used to tell my husband. Women smell of oil lamps and cook fires, while men smell like the olive groves they tend, or the wheat they thresh. He smelled like new-mown hay; the aroma reminded me of my husband, and I could not keep the tears from my cheeks. He picked me up and I clung to him, all the stress and worry of the past years leaving my body through tears and deep sobs. He held me while I cried, stroking my hair and murmuring soothing reassurances. When the tears ceased and my breathing slowed, he still held me, his strong arms a bulwark against my fears.

He left before daylight, hoping no one would see his departure. I tried to behave normally that day, but how does one behave after breaking Yahweh's law? I was silent, but my friends were used to my silence by now, and chattered amongst themselves, leaving me in peace.

Only I was not peaceful. I kept replaying the day before in my mind, rehearsing every action, every word, every thought. I told myself I should be ashamed, should be disgusted with myself, but I was not. I felt loved and cared about. In fact, I half-hoped he would visit me again.

My house was empty that night, and for several nights after that I wept into my pillow until I had no more tears, and slid into slumber. Sleep brought no peace, either. Images of golden calves and stone tablets invaded my dreams. Some nights I was in the Red Sea with Pharaoh's chariots, drowning when Yahweh released the waters. Another night, the Angel of Death stalked me through the streets of my village, as he stalked the first-born so long ago. All doors were closed to me, the people safely locked inside protected by the lamb's blood on the lintels, while I stayed outside, unprotected.

The worst was the night I saw Moshe descending the mountain, cradling the tablets of Yahweh's law to his chest. The golden calf shone in the firelight as he came near the camp. When Moshe threw the tablets away in his rage, they floated towards me. I was frozen in place, unable to move, unable even to scream, until I crashed into blackness.

After *that* dream, I promised Yahweh I would obey. I would stop thinking of this man, stop remembering our night together. I would probably never see him again anyway. It had been a full month since he had left me in the early morning, and it was obvious he had no real interest in me, so my promise to Yahweh was not difficult to make.

That very night, when it was full dark, he returned, slipping into the house unexpectedly.

"I had to come back," he said, "to see if you were as beautiful as I remembered." He crossed the room to where I stood motionless, staring at him.

"You *are* beautiful."

My promise to Yahweh drowned in the tide of pleasure I felt as he embraced me.

I will not say the nightmares never returned, but they were not as frequent, and never again as vivid as the night I was crushed under the tablets of the law. My friend also returned, each time swearing he was captivated by my beauty, that he only felt alive when he was with me.

By the time I learned he was married, it did not matter. What mattered was the way I felt when he was with me, reminding me of the way I felt when my husband was alive. He was the first man since my husband who made me feel cared about, and desirable.

He was not the last.

The first few times, I tried to resist, but the need to feel loved and desirable proved stronger than my forgotten promise to Yahweh. No, my promise wasn't really forgotten. When I slept alone, it echoed through my nightmares. If I did not sleep alone, it became the sledgehammer I used each day to remind myself how terrible I was. My friends abandoned me, unwilling to associate with an adulteress.

Adulteress: there's a word I never thought would be used to describe me. At least my parents were dead, and could not share my shame. Shame, guilt, condemnation…these were my feelings after seeking comfort in someone's arms yet again. Those were the days when I hated myself for not being strong enough to resist temptation.

But when I was alone, with no one nearby to tempt me, I
felt abandoned and unloved, angry at Yahweh for taking
my husband and my parents, for leaving me alone and
vulnerable to this body hunger. Sometimes I wished I had
never married: if I had not known how pleasant a man's
caresses could be, I would not miss them. But I had been
married and I did miss the comfort of my husband's love,
so I continued to make those bad choices, pretending these
other men actually cared for me, not just for how I made
them feel.

Bad choices can kill you, and I almost died today. I was
asleep with a companion, and did not hear the commotion
outside until the door burst open, broken almost in two by
the force they used. Several men rushed in, shouting
commands. We were barely given time to dress before
they dragged us out into the street.

A crowd gathered to watch the spectacle we made as they
pushed and pulled us along to the Temple. I remember the
stars just fading out of the sky, the dry desert dust puffing
up around us as we half-walked, half-ran with our captors.
What faces I could see in the crowd showed no
compassion, only joy at our predicament. But the faces of
our accusers – those I knew. I had seen those faces other
times, other circumstances, and wondered what had
happened to cause this change in them today.

I suddenly realized that I was the only one being dragged
along. My companion had melted into the crowd, and was
now shouting curses at me, instead of telling me how
beautiful I was.

As we neared the Temple, the Pharisees and other teachers
came out to join us, directing our path to the courts. I saw a
man sitting there, speaking to some people gathered around
him. Someone grabbed my wrist and half-flung me in front
of him, laughing when I stumbled and almost fell. Rough

hands set me upright, while rough voices told this teacher my sins, and reminded him that Moshe said I should be stoned.

Stoned! My heart almost stopped. Surely I did not deserve to be stoned! I had done nothing but try and find solace in my misery, while providing comfort to others who were miserable.

The accusations continued, angry voices growling my offenses, sharing details that could only be known to me or my companions. I stared at the ground, not wanting to look up, not wanting to see the faces of former friends and former companions distorted by the hatred I heard in their voices.

In my mind, I saw the tablets from my nightmare floating towards me, implacable and irresistible.

"Not me," I pleaded silently. *"I am not an adulteress – just a lonely woman."* The men I had known appeared before me. I was shocked at their number. Had there really been that many? Then I realized the men were not alone. Their wives and children appeared with them, and then the men faded, leaving only the families. The women looked sad, eyes puffy from crying. I heard the children asking why their fathers weren't home, and saw the mothers blink away tears before changing the topic.

I blinked and the families melted away, leaving me staring at the sand, knowing my accusers were correct: I *should* be stoned. I had no defense, and resigned myself to my fate. Any minute now, this teacher would confirm their judgment. I would be dragged outside the city; my former friends and companions would ring themselves around me, and stones would begin to fly towards me, seeking to crush me for my sins.

"Yahweh," I whispered silently, *"I know I don't deserve your mercy, but please let one of those rocks hit me in the head very quickly."*

But no one grabbed me to drag me away. Instead, I heard their angry voices again, demanding a response from this new teacher. I dared to look at him – he was simply drawing pictures in the sand with his finger. I looked away before he could see me, staring at the ground again, wondering what he was drawing. His words silenced them, and I heard the shuffle of feet as the crowd slowly left.

When it was just the two of us, he rose and looked at me, and I at him.

"Where are your accusers?" he asked quietly, no anger or judgment in his voice.

I looked around, amazed that not even one of the crowd had stayed. But one accuser still remained. I was accused, tried, and convicted within my own heart.

His eyes gazing into mine were warm and caring. As I searched them for the condemnation I knew must be there, I saw again the tablets of the law flying toward me at dizzying speed, getting larger as they grew nearer. Yahweh's law proclaimed me guilty. I knew it, he knew it, and I waited to hear him say it.

He smiled at me, and the tablets shattered. They were no longer granite stones seeking to break my body apart, just grains of sand falling to the ground in front of me.

I looked at him, not daring to believe what I had seen. Not daring to hope that I was free. He smiled again, and I saw in his eyes the love I had sought in all those other encounters.

His command to me seemed almost impossible given my past, but bolstered by the love I saw in his eyes, I knew this time I could obey.